I0491866

THANK YOU FOR YOUR PURCHASE

I hope you enjoy this coloring book.
May in bring you peace and relaxation.
To find other great products
visit TerryHelliker.com.

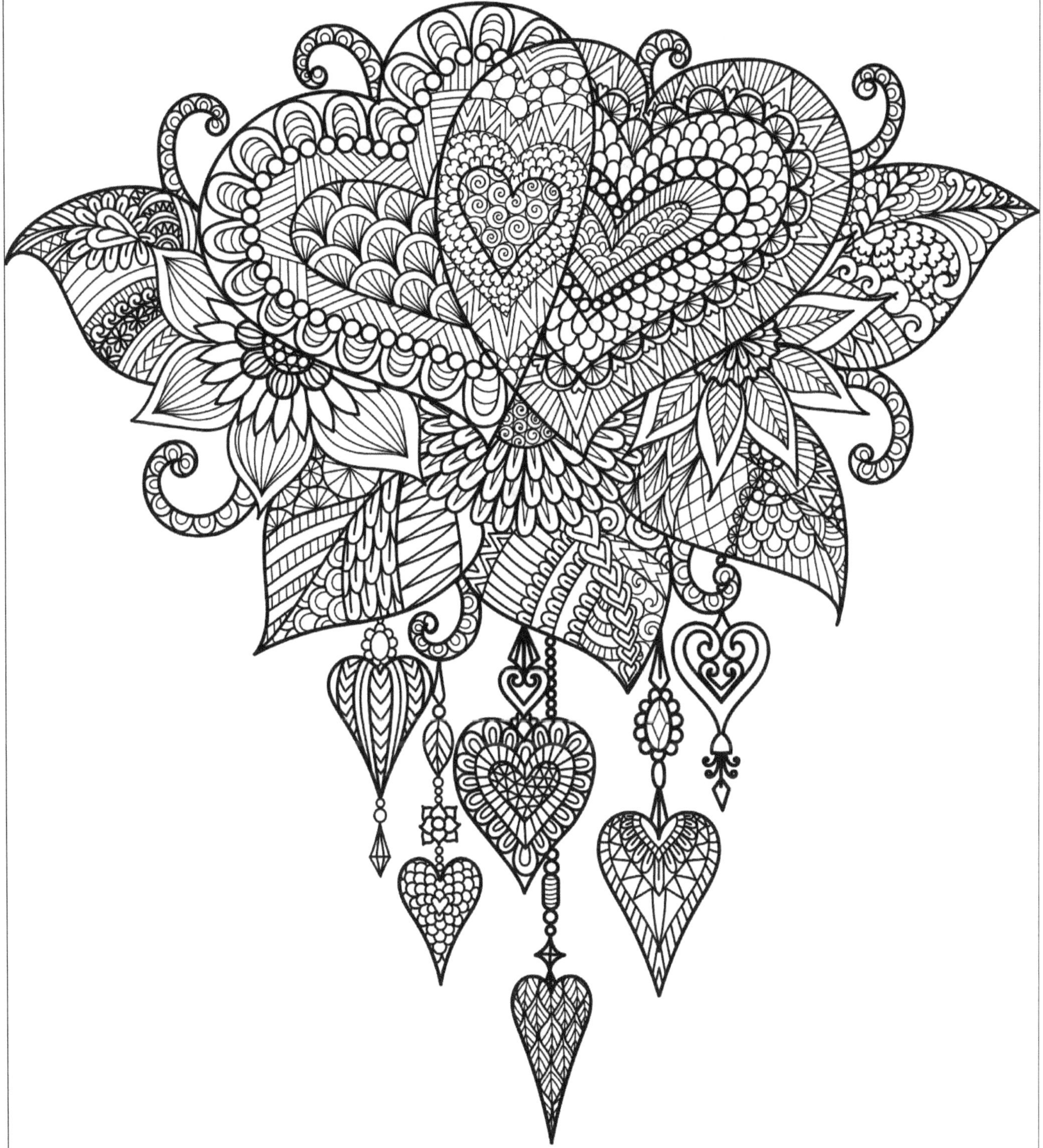

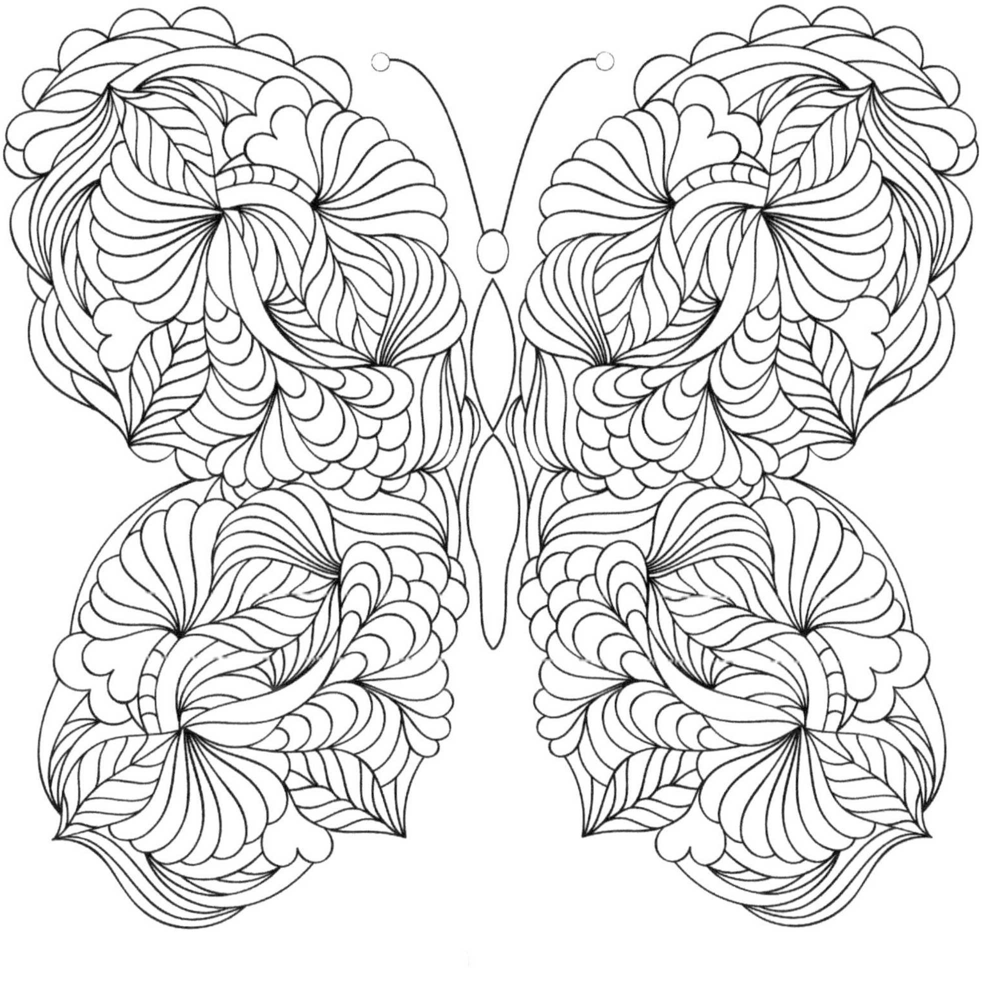

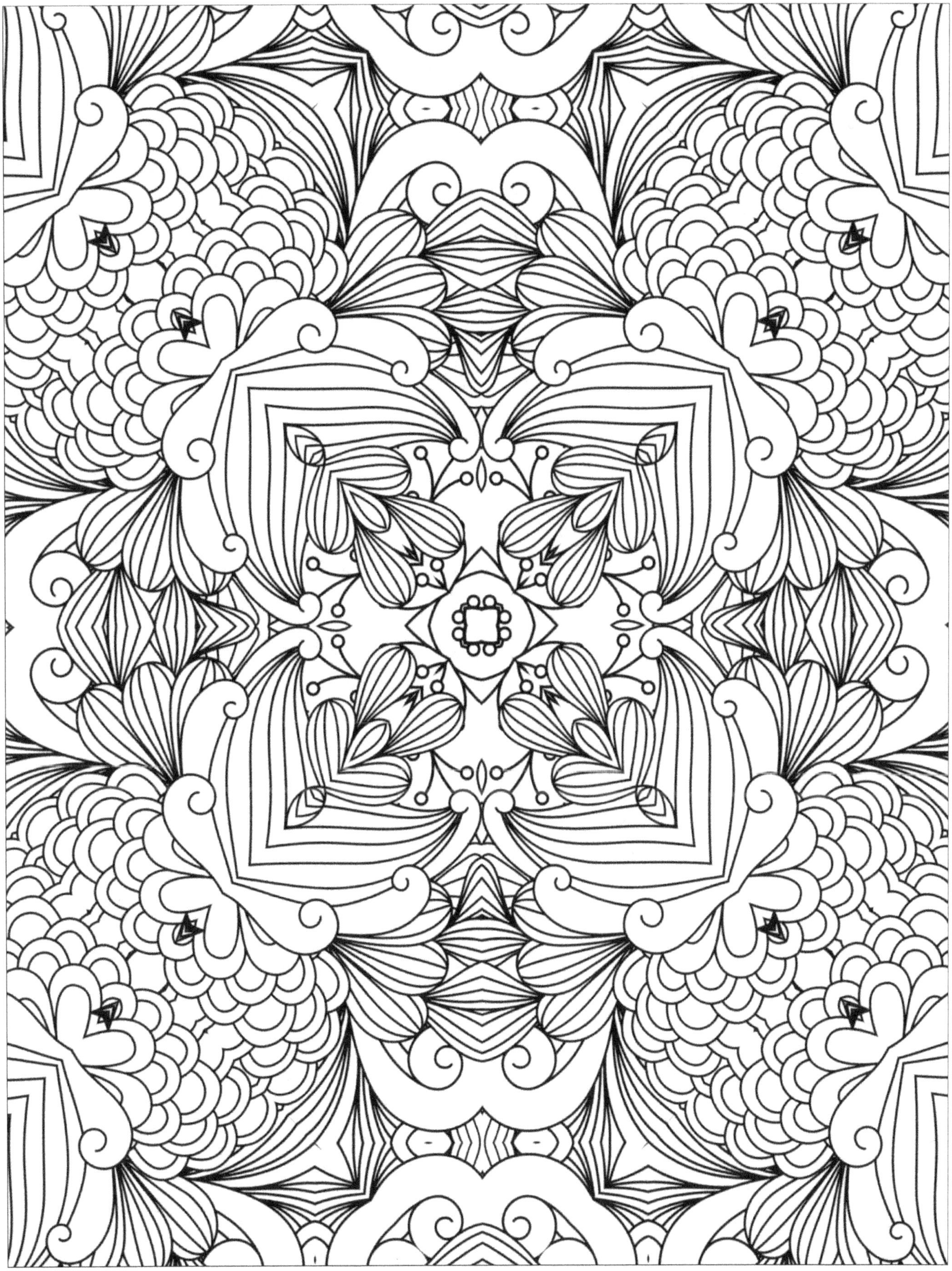

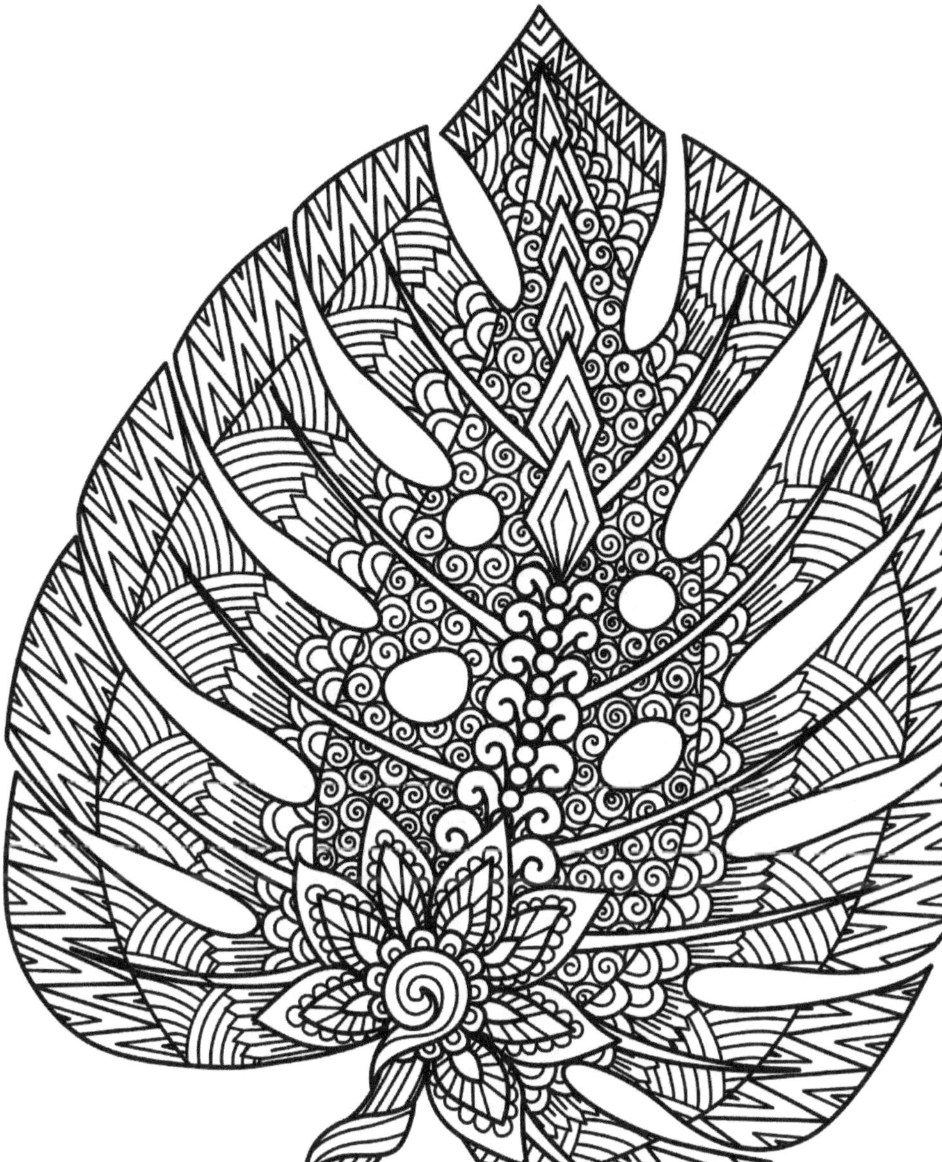

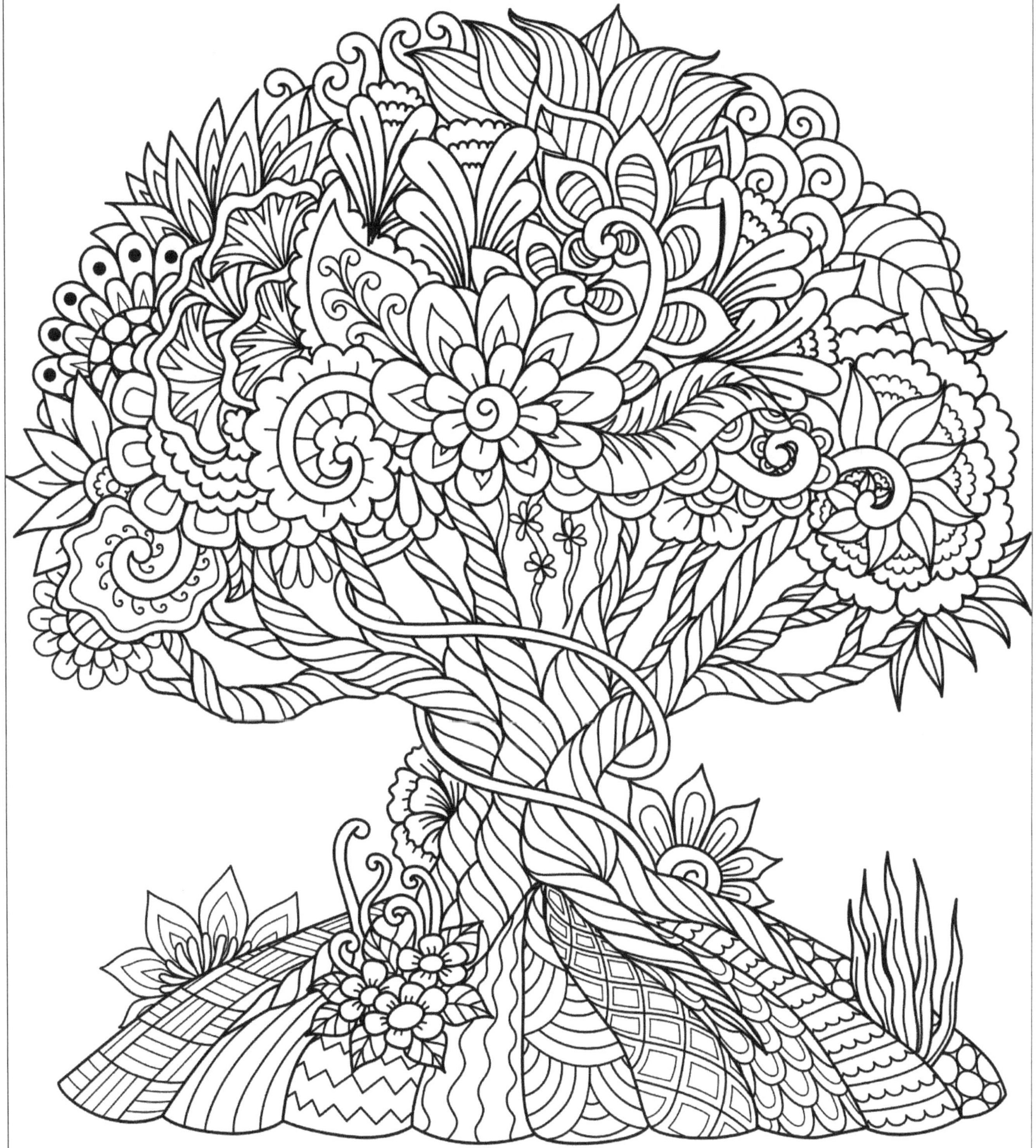

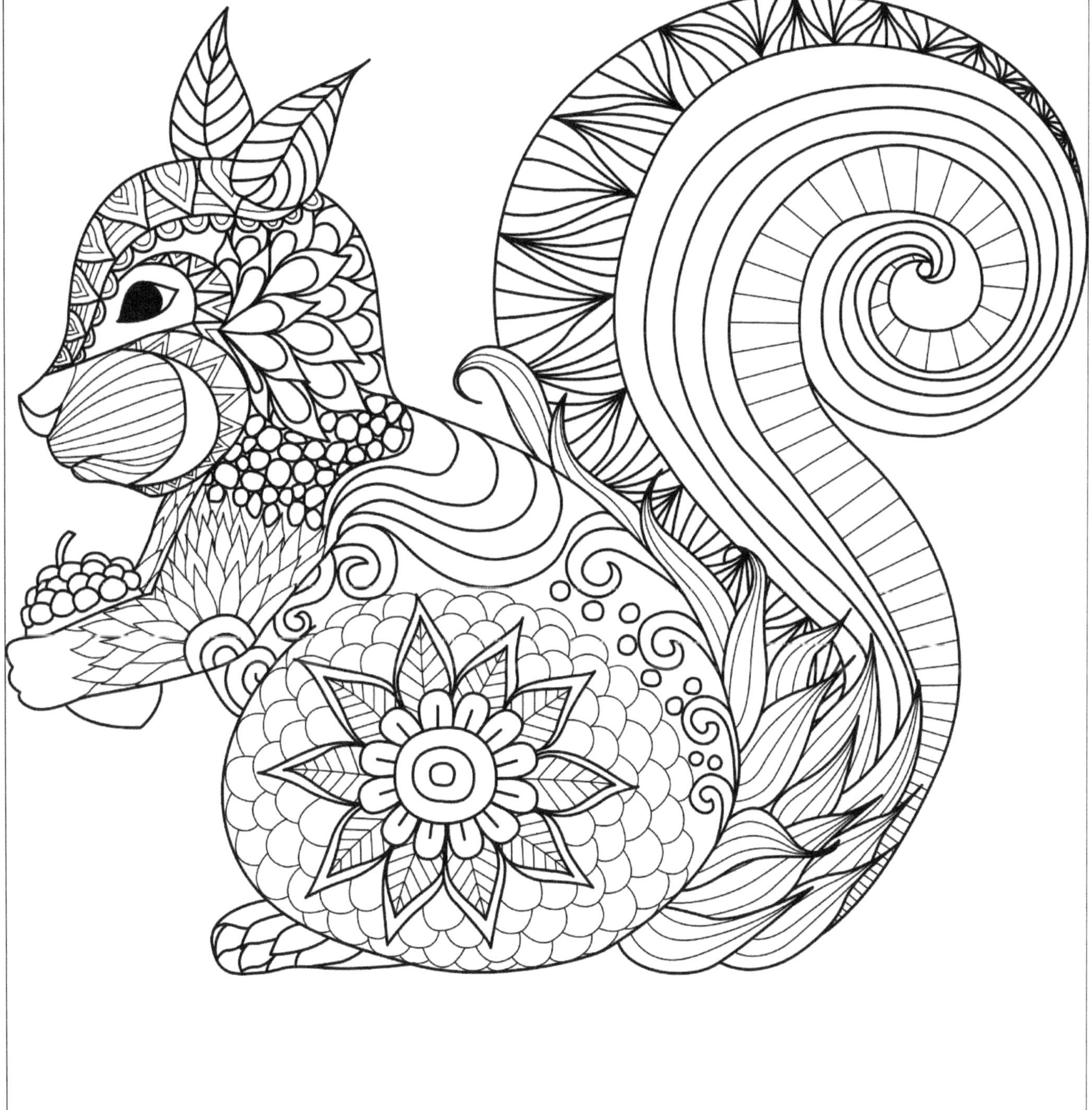

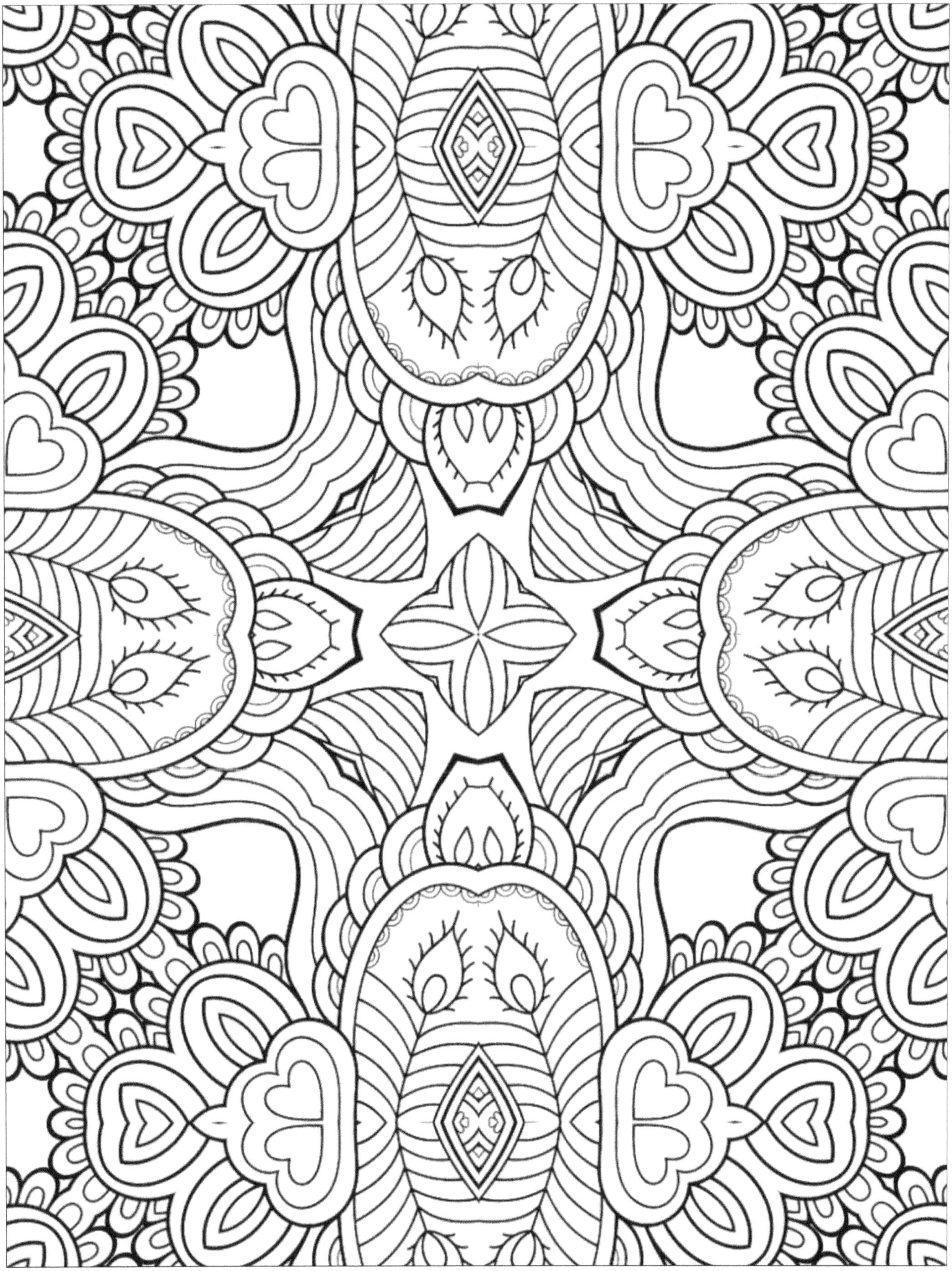

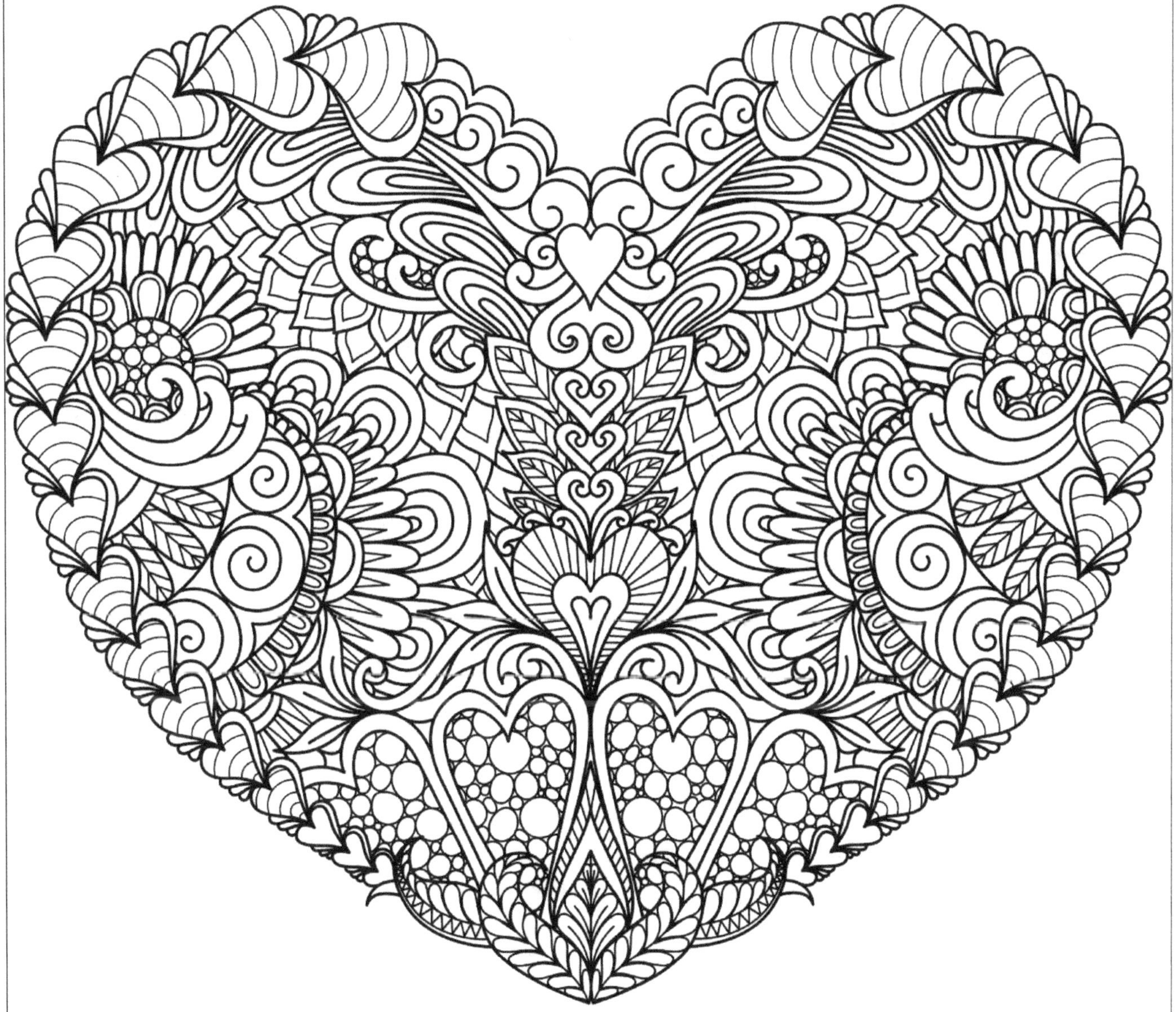

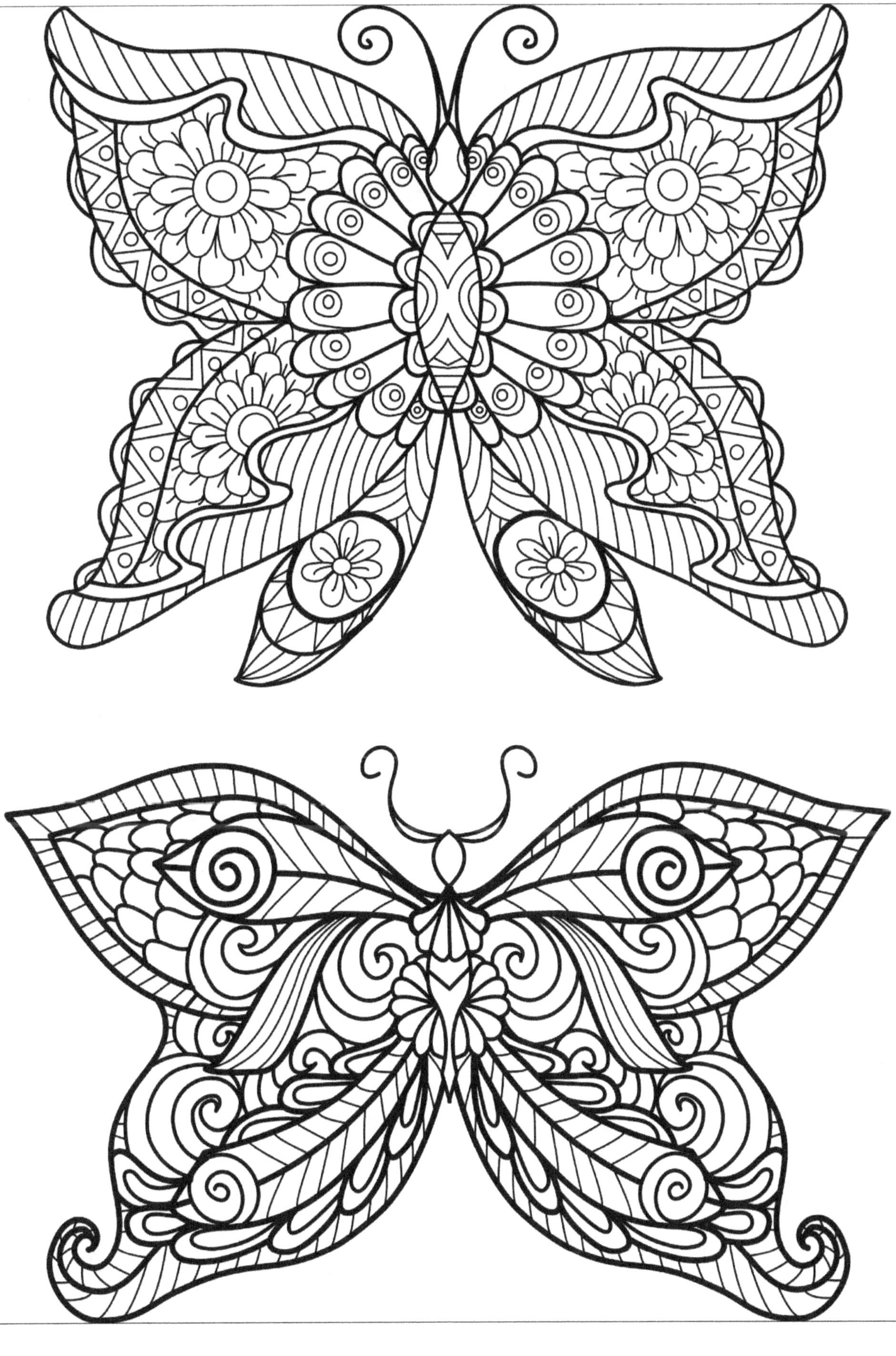

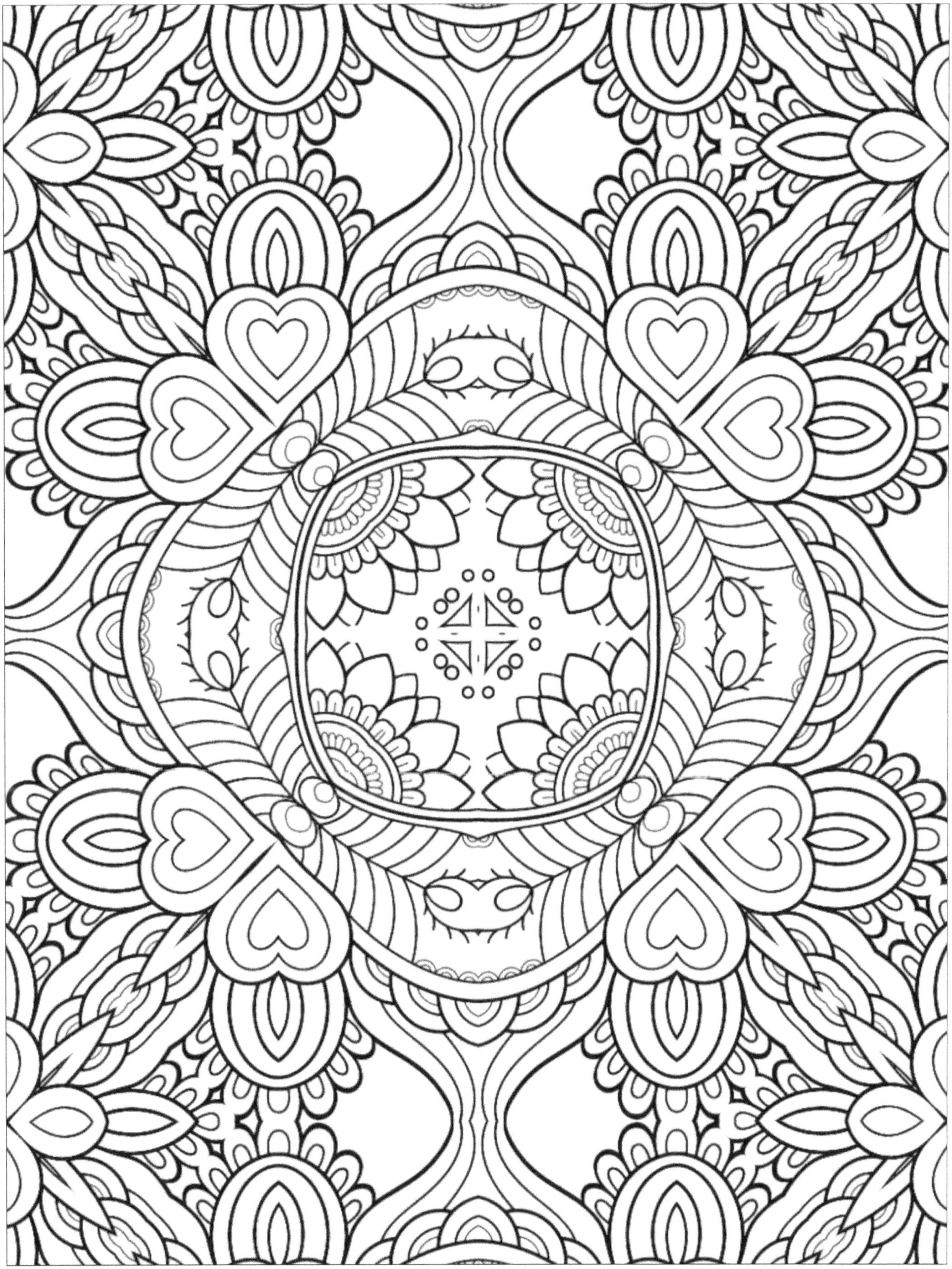

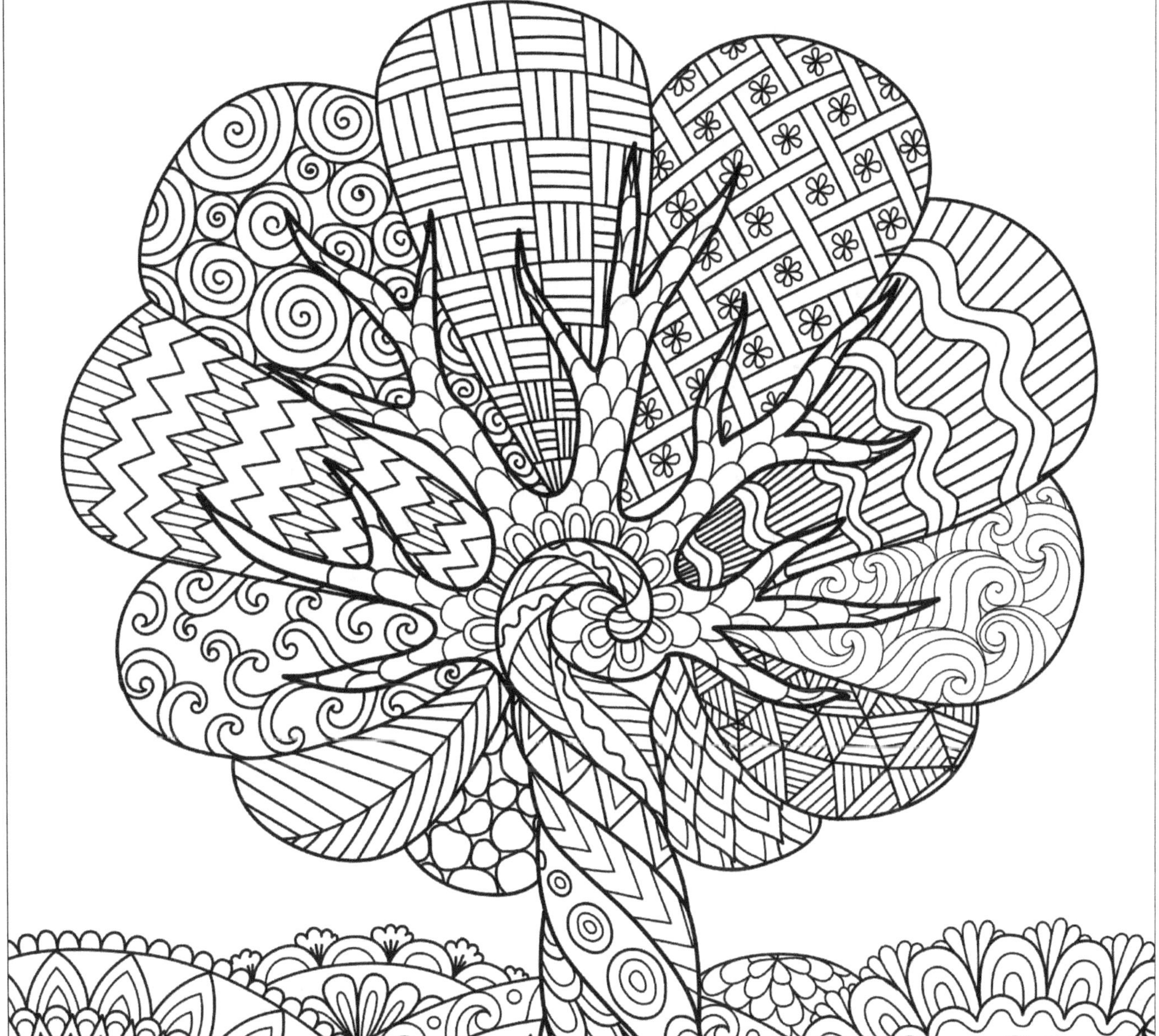

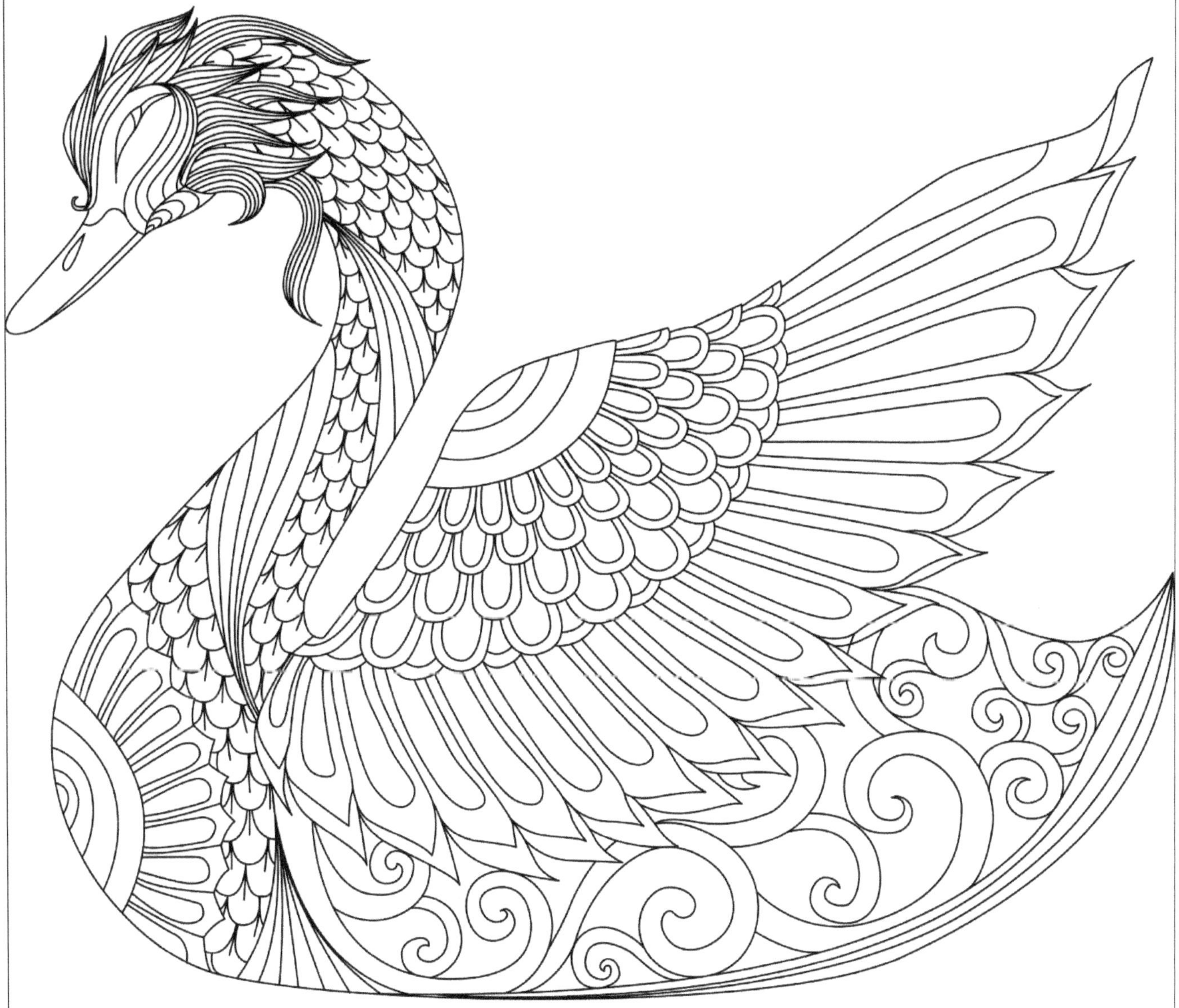

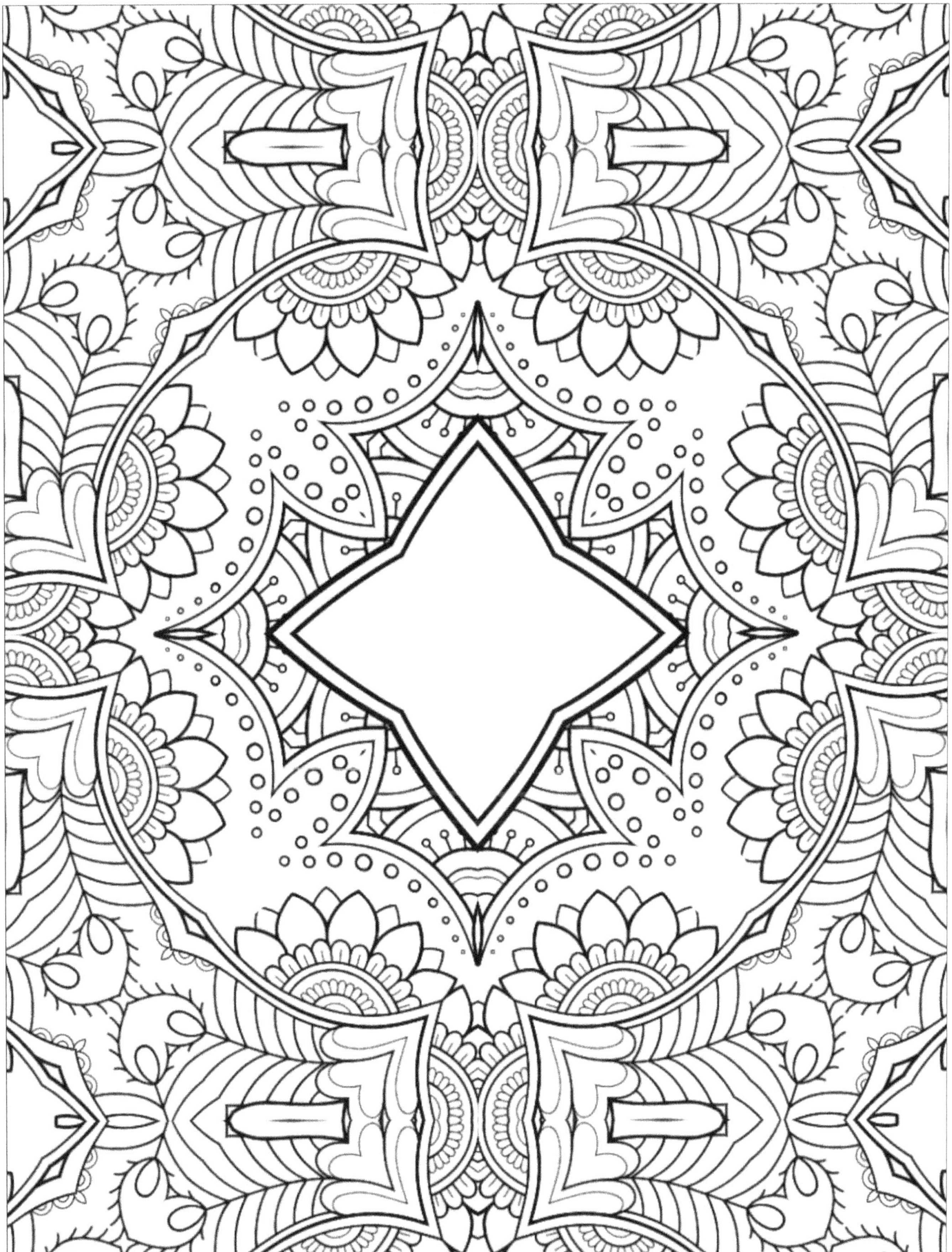

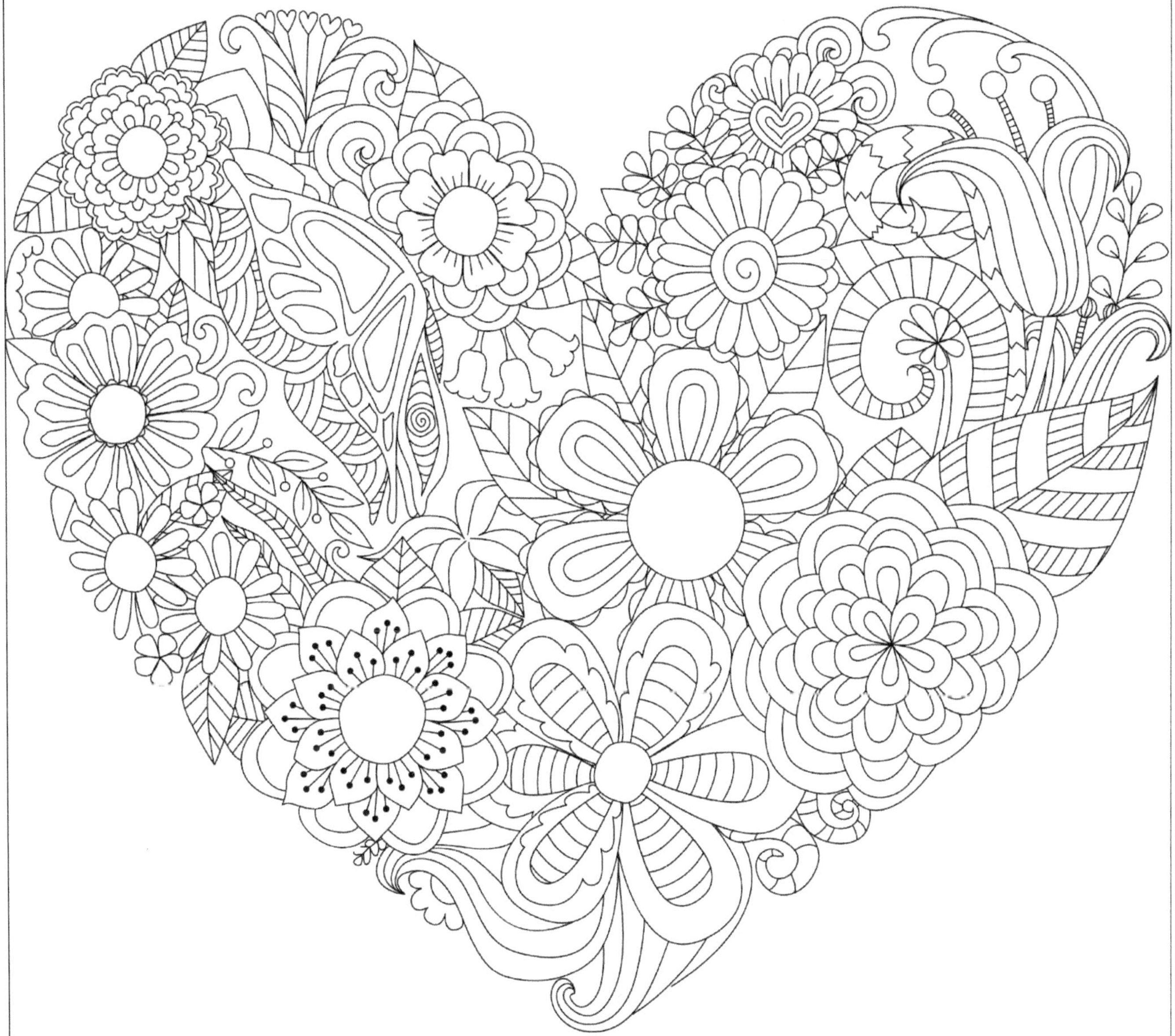

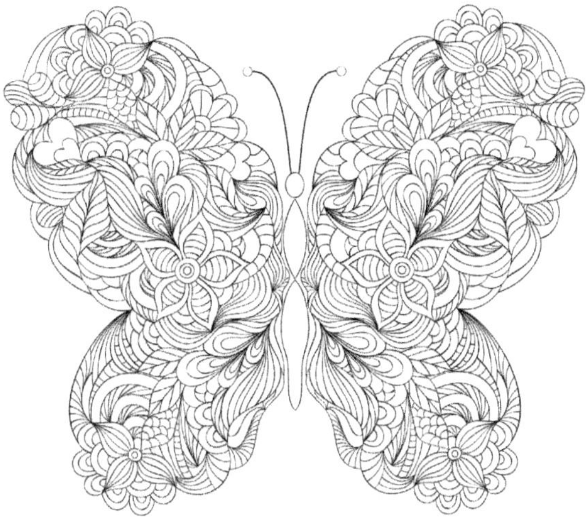
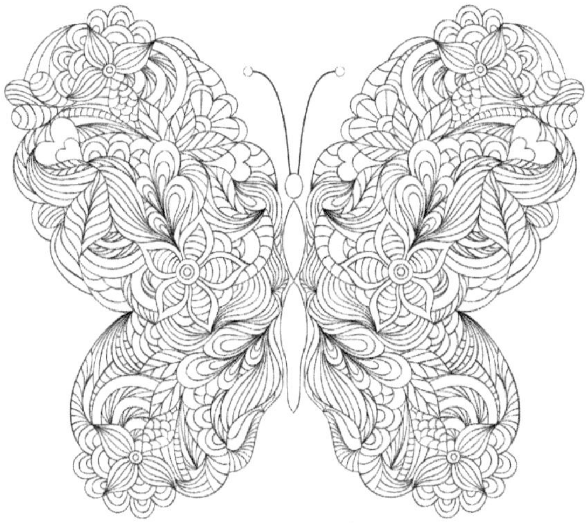
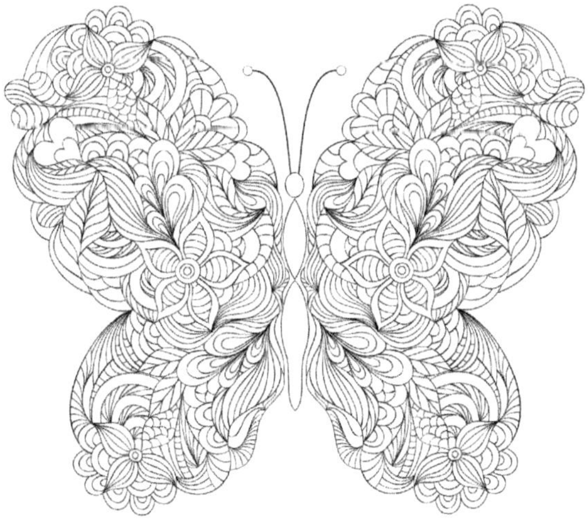
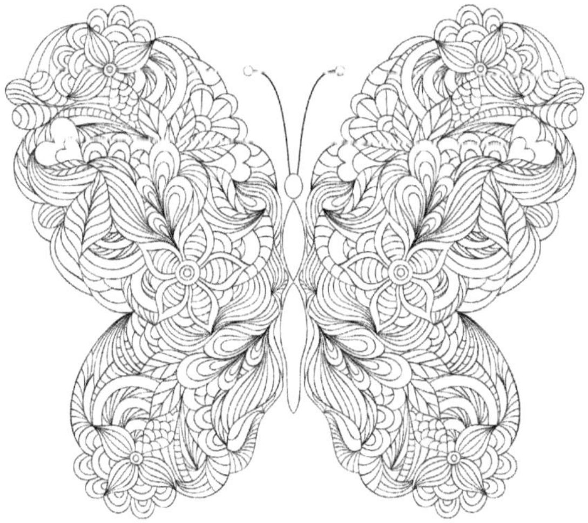

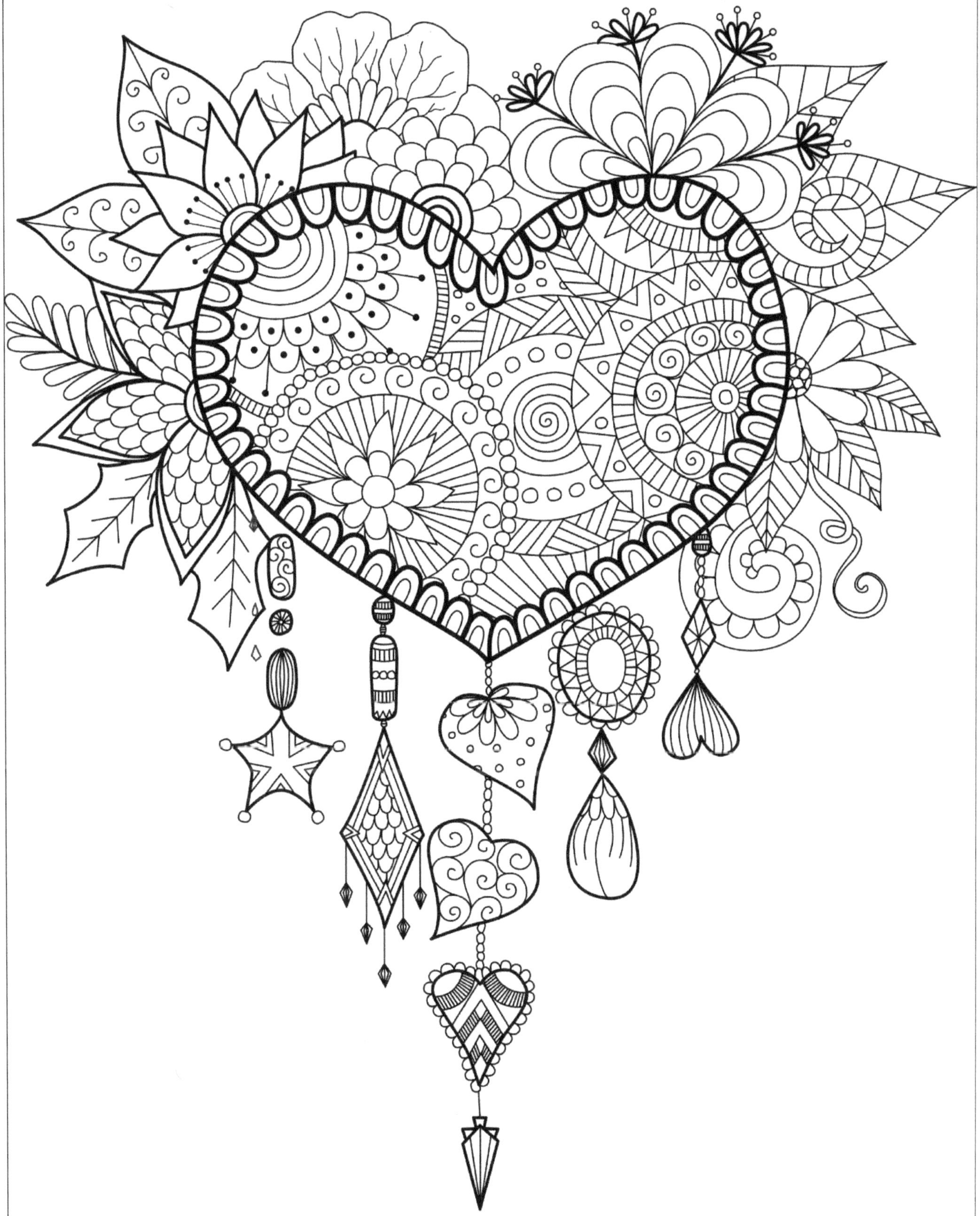

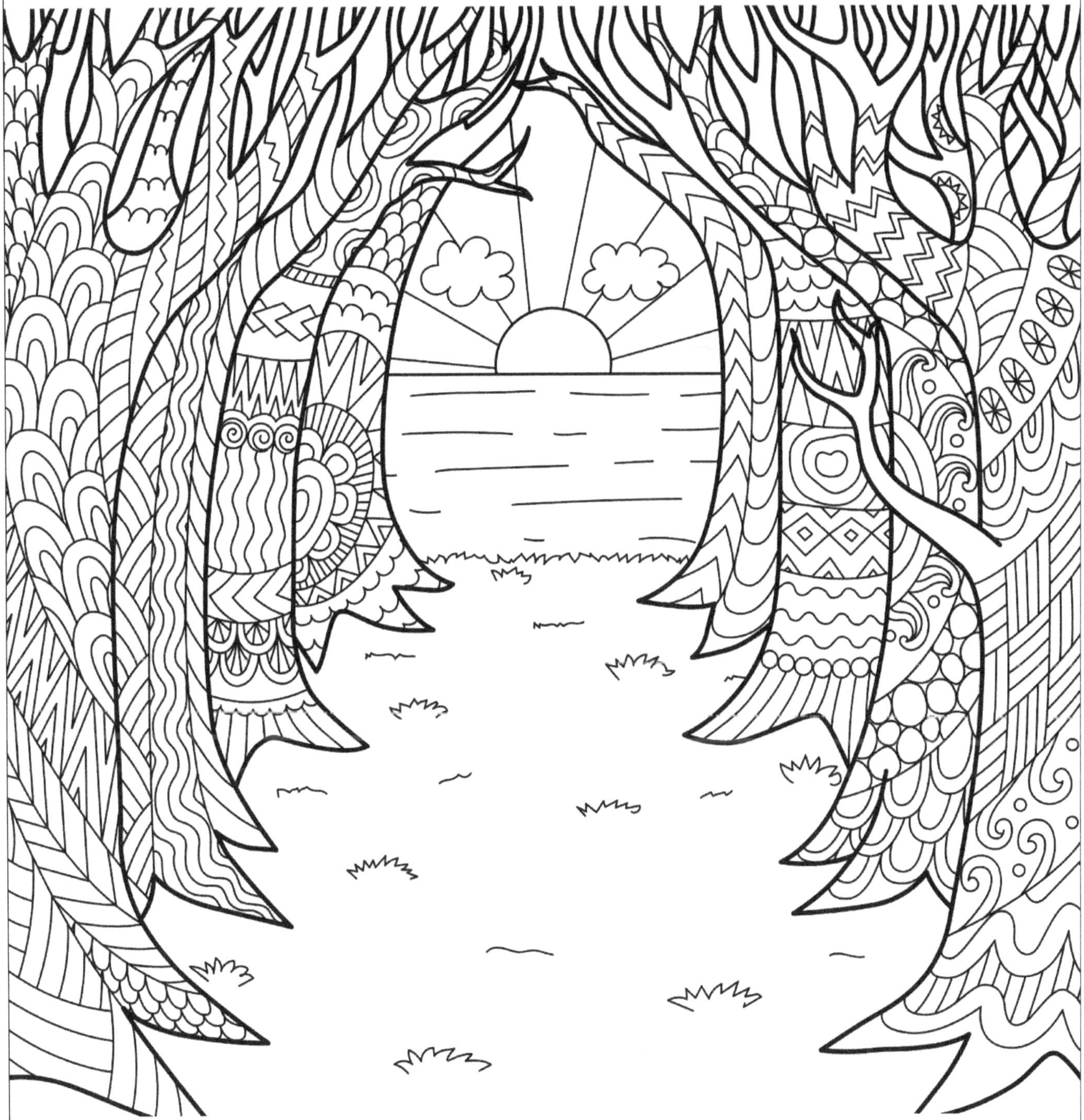

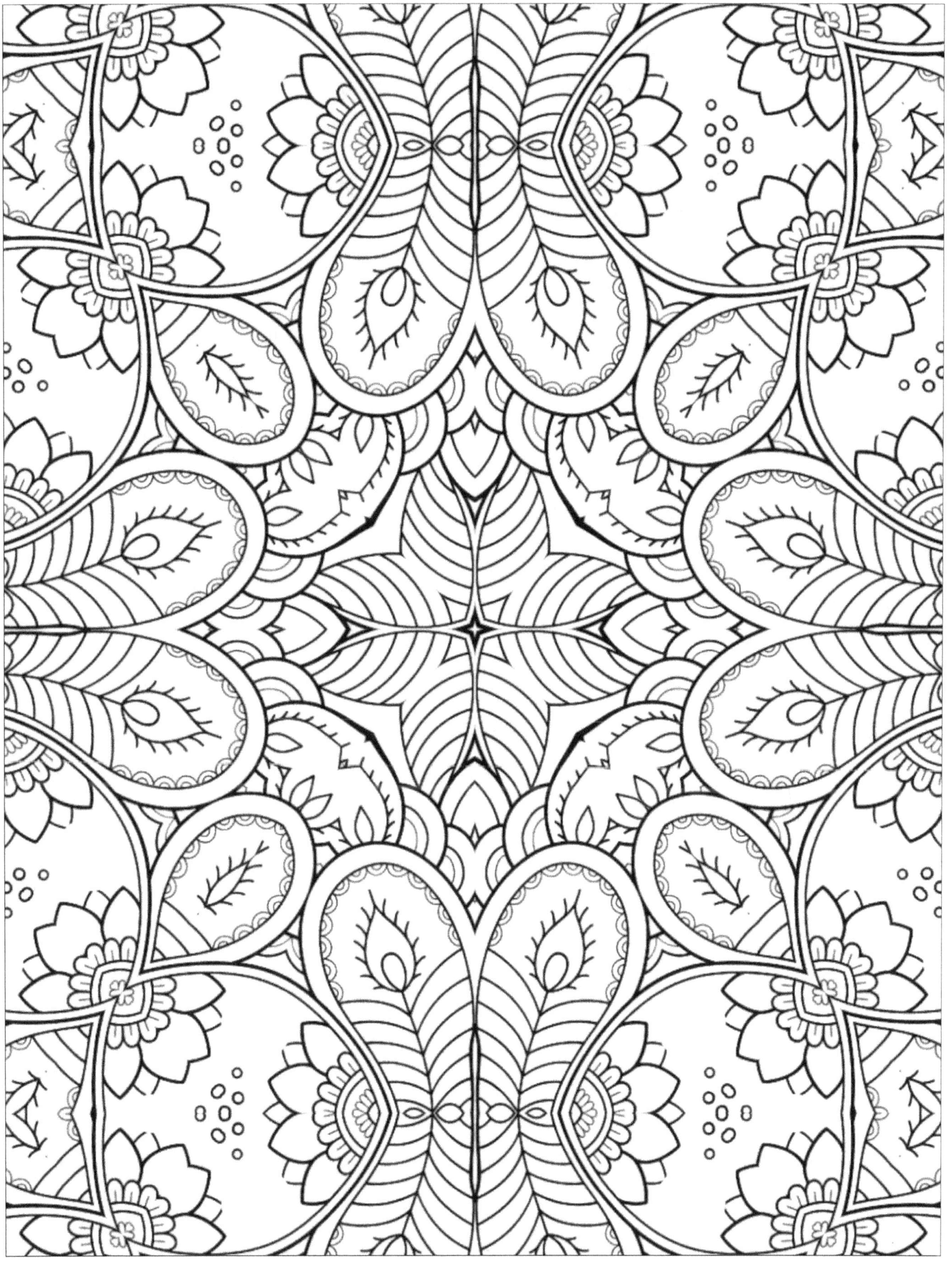

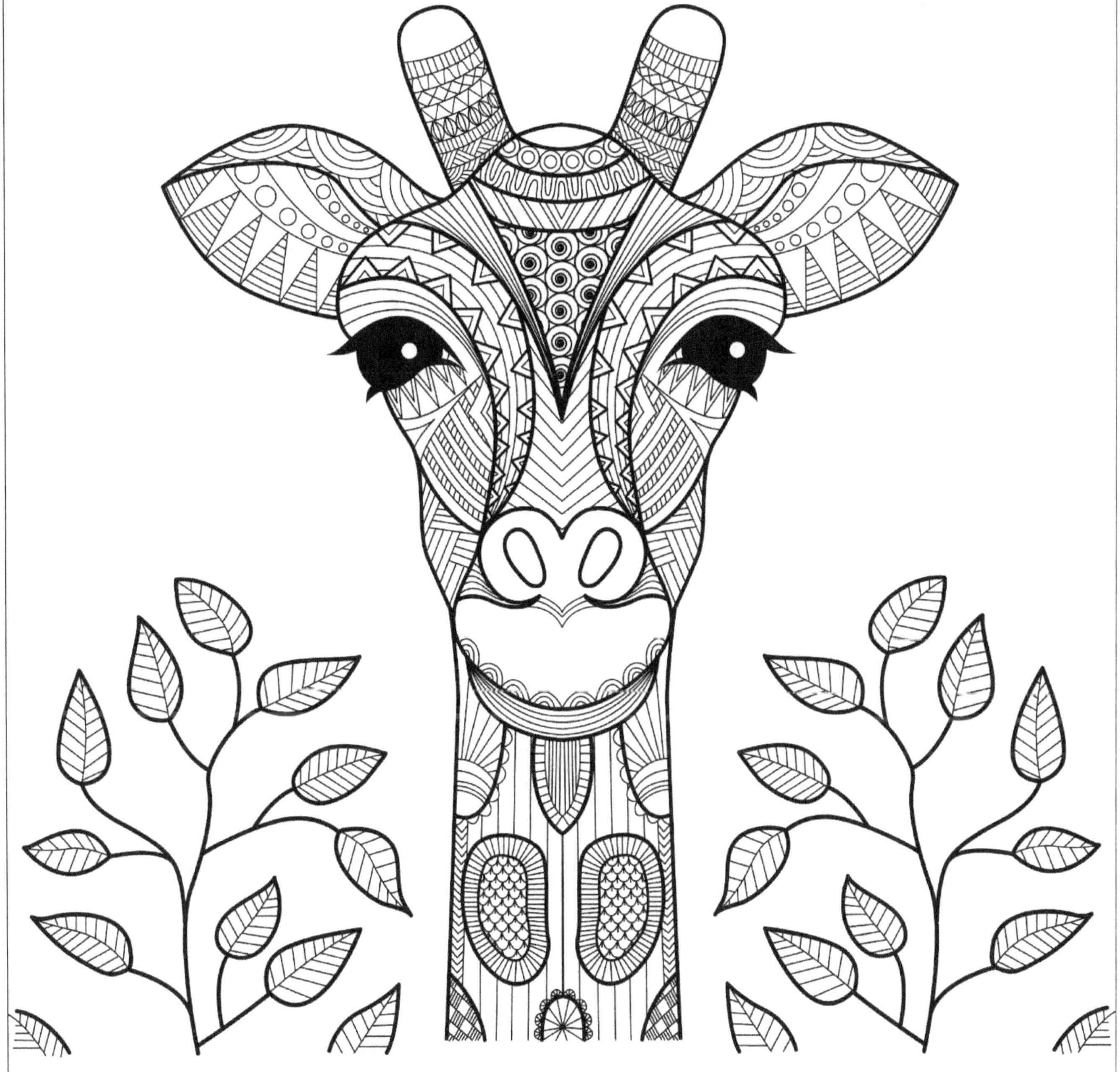

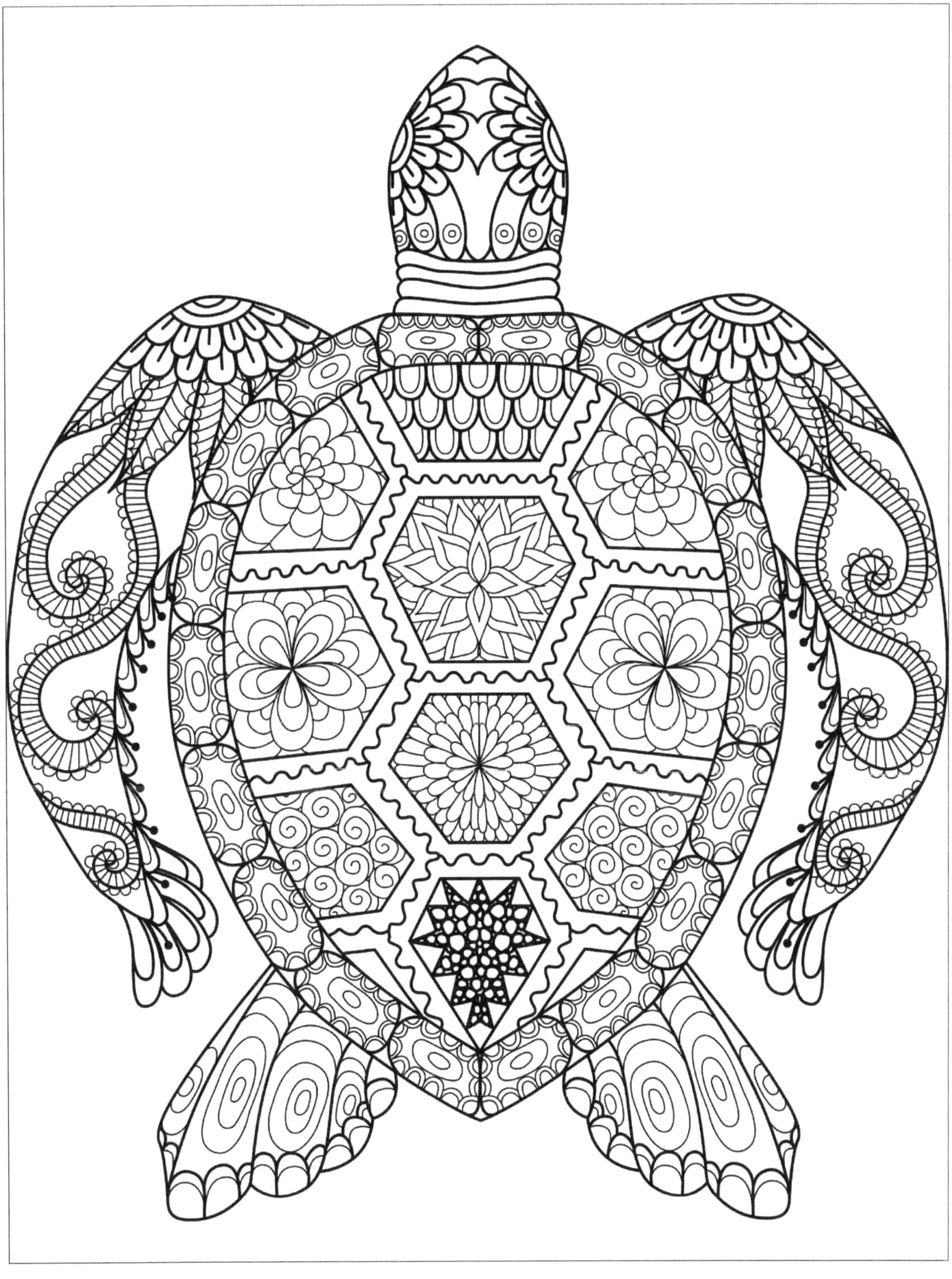

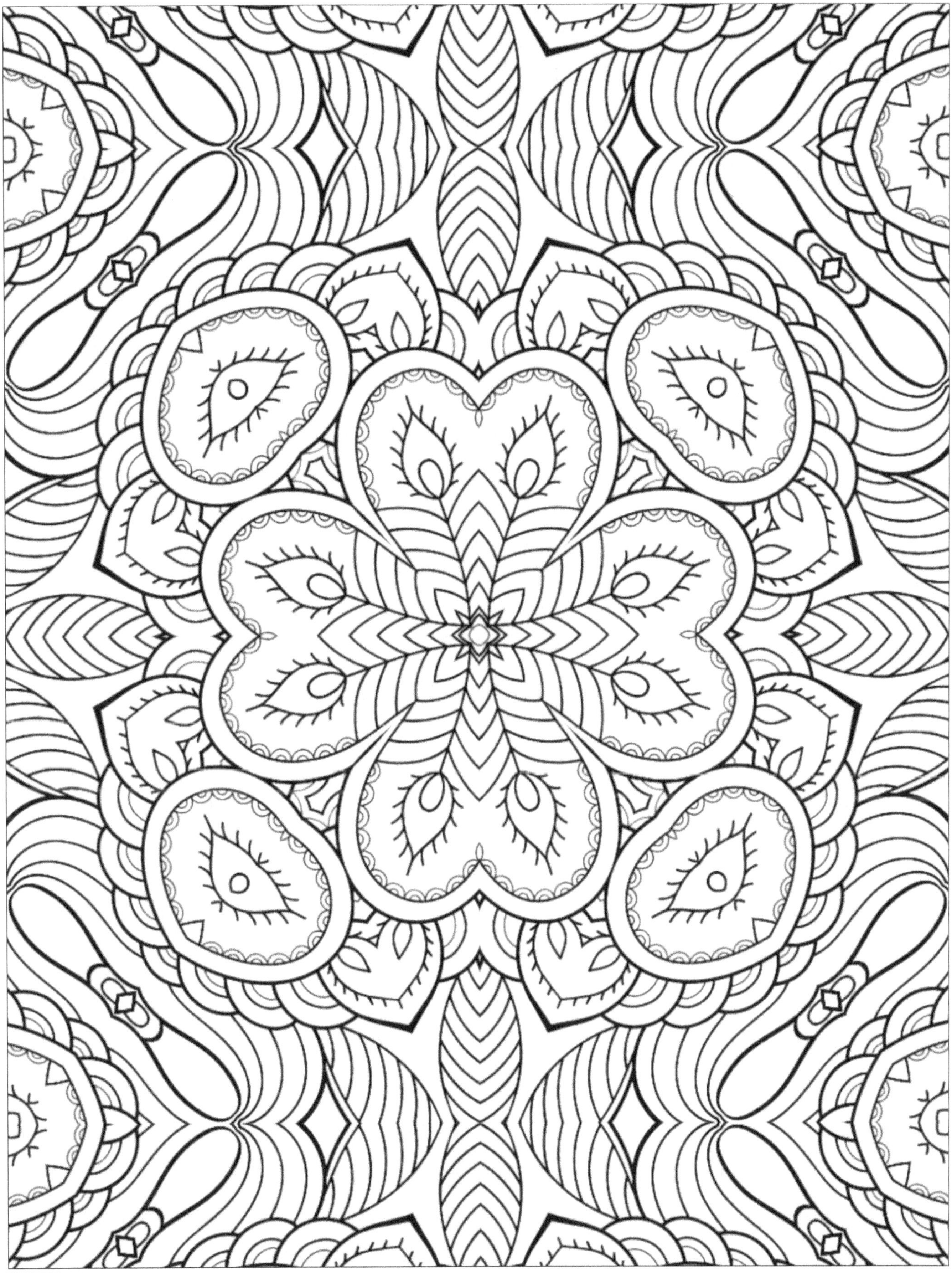

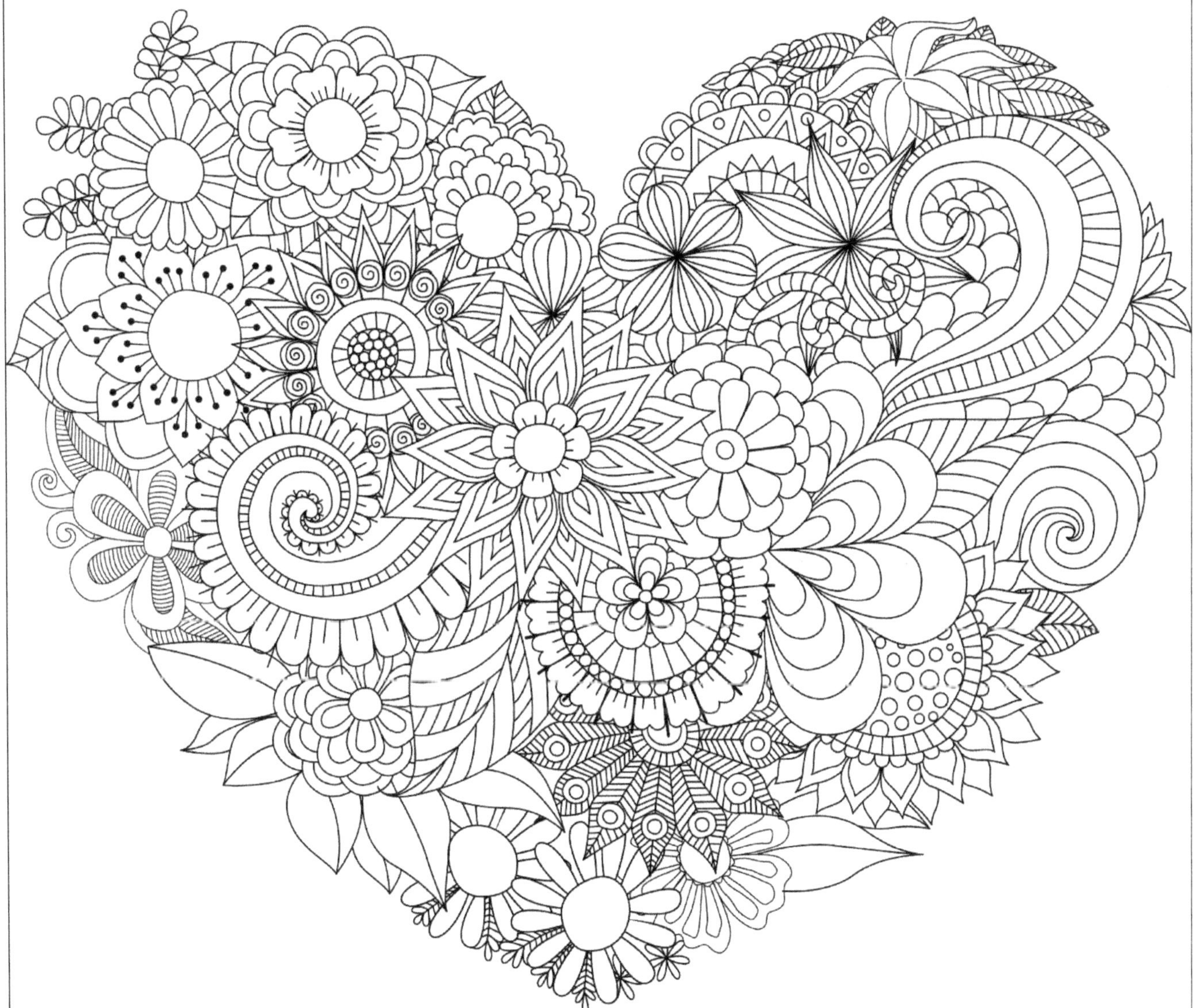

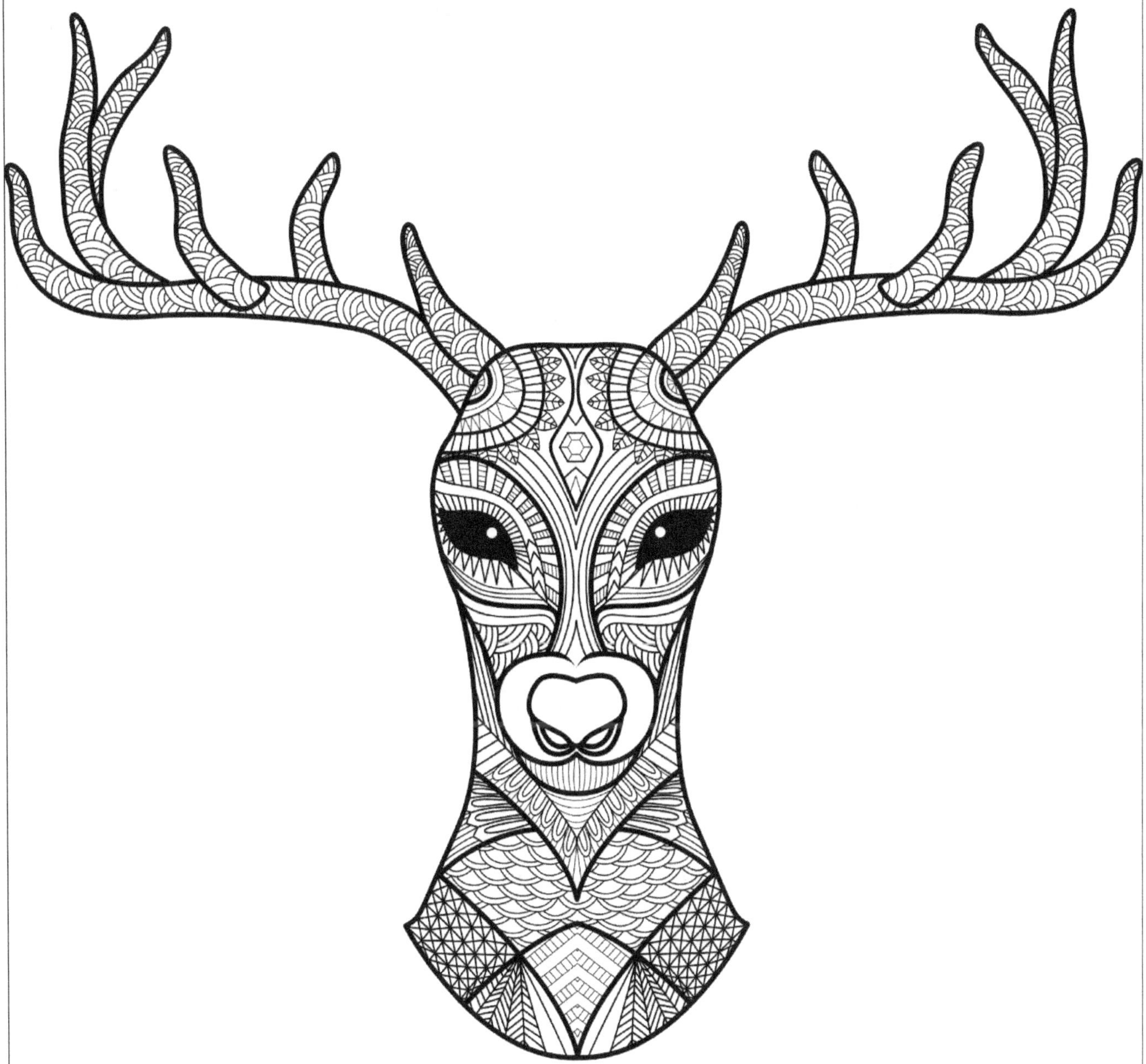

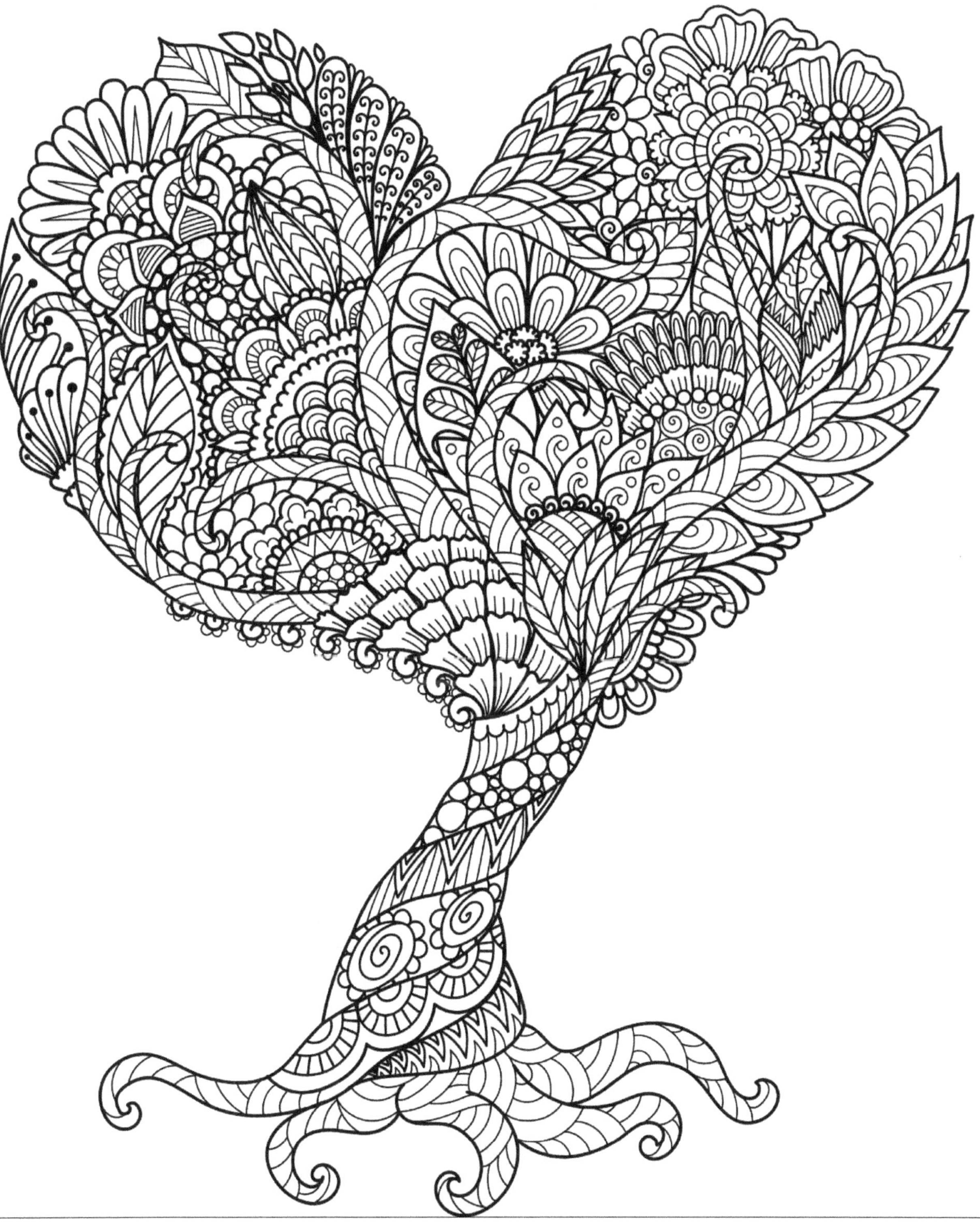

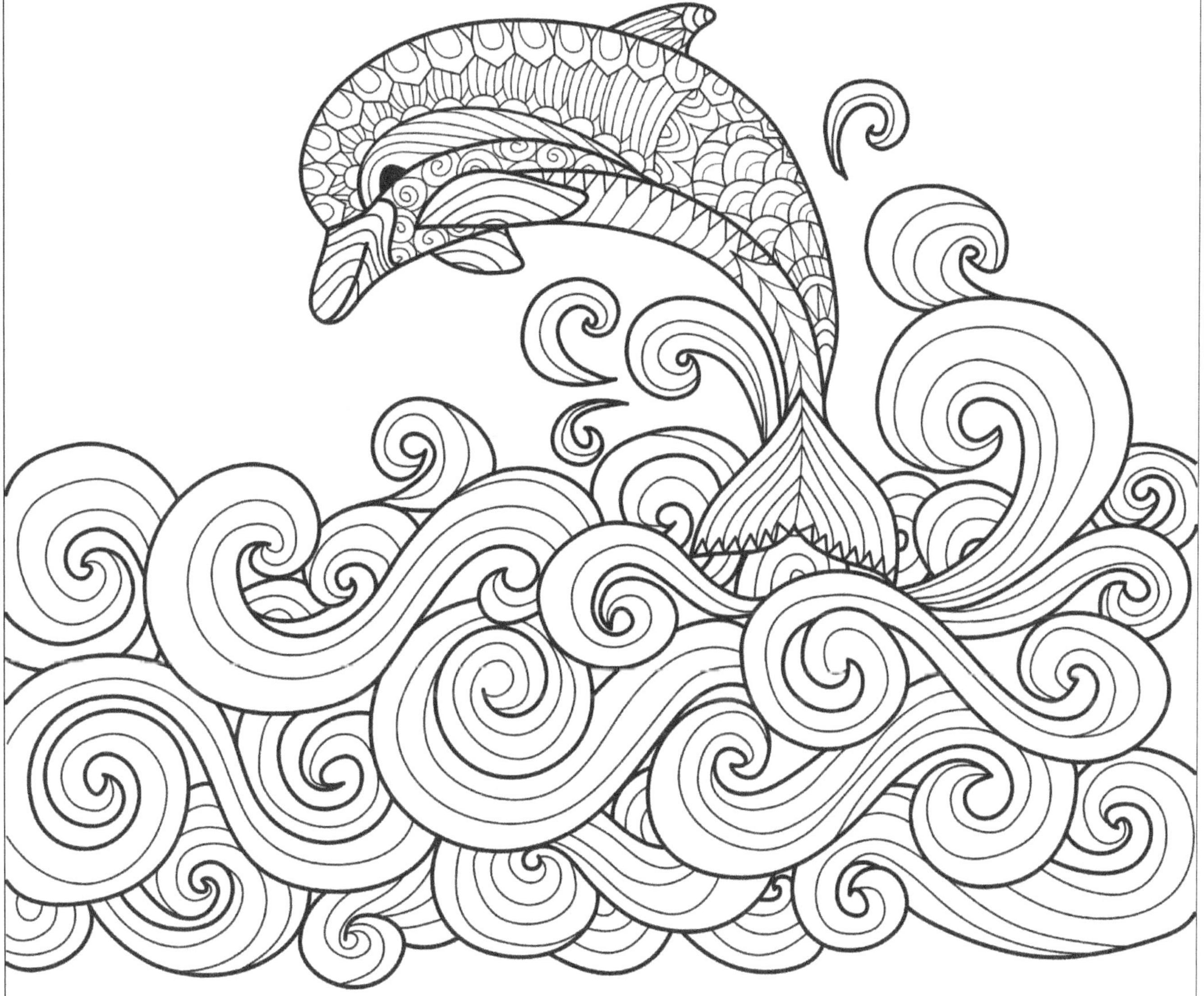

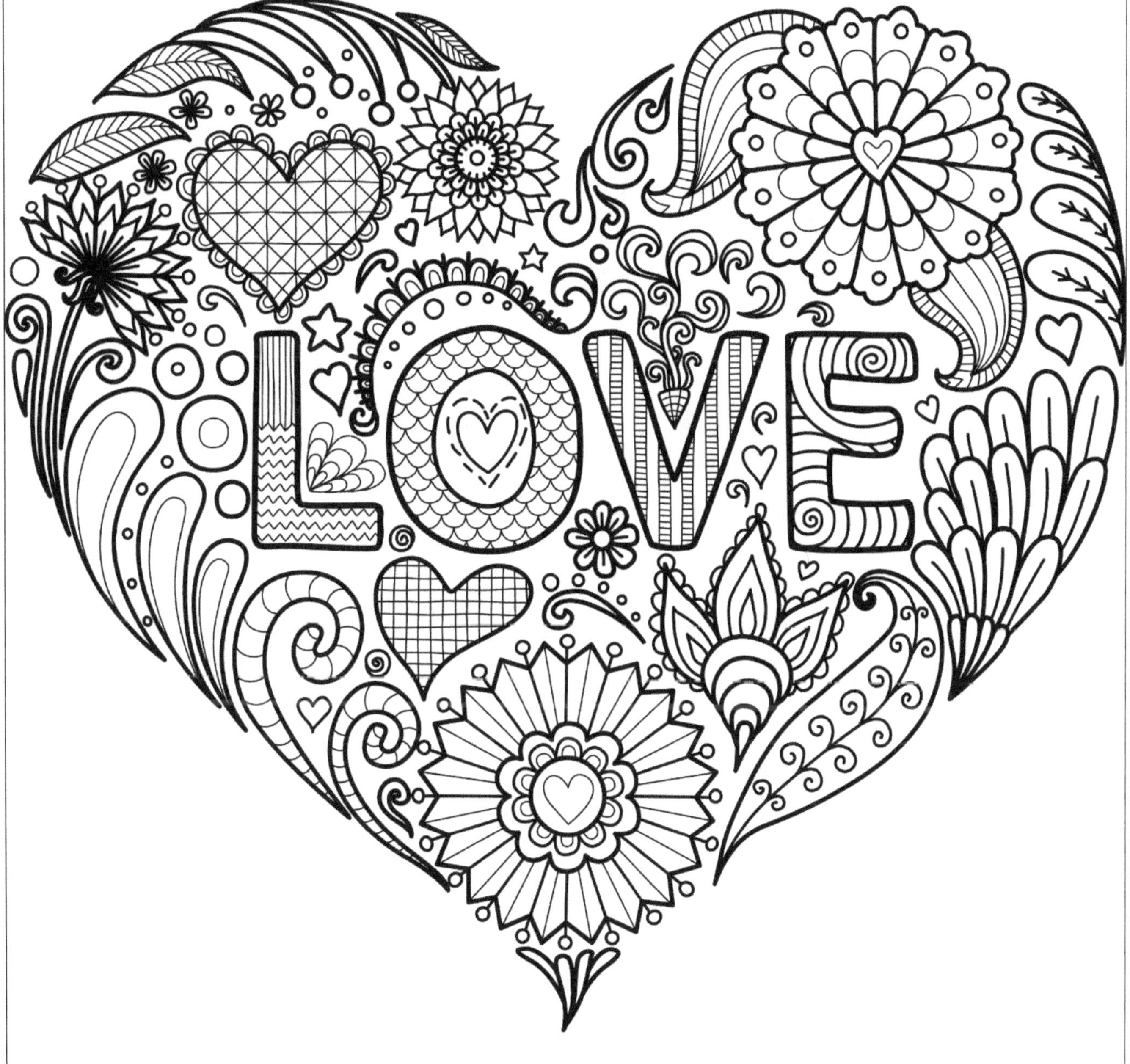
LOVE

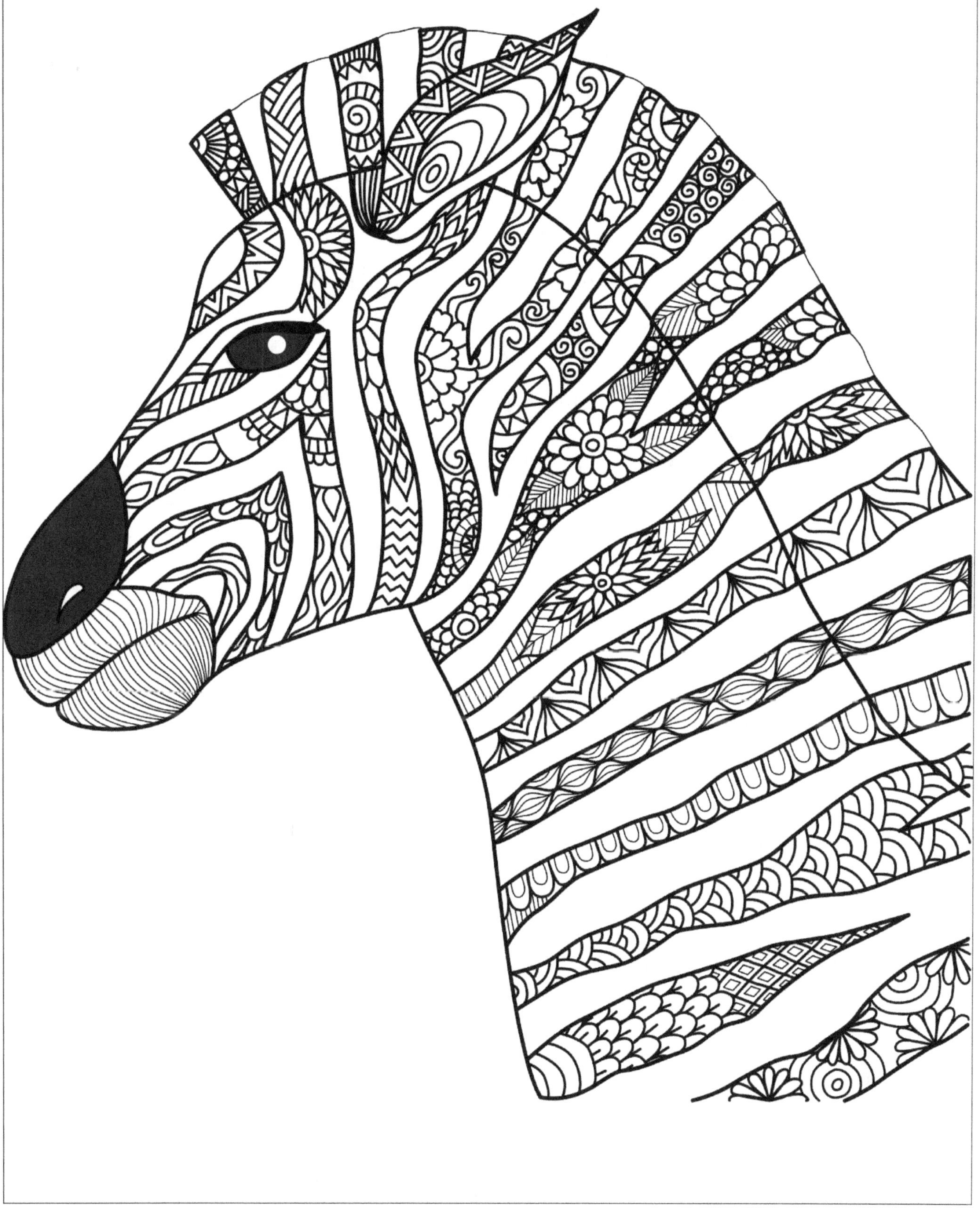

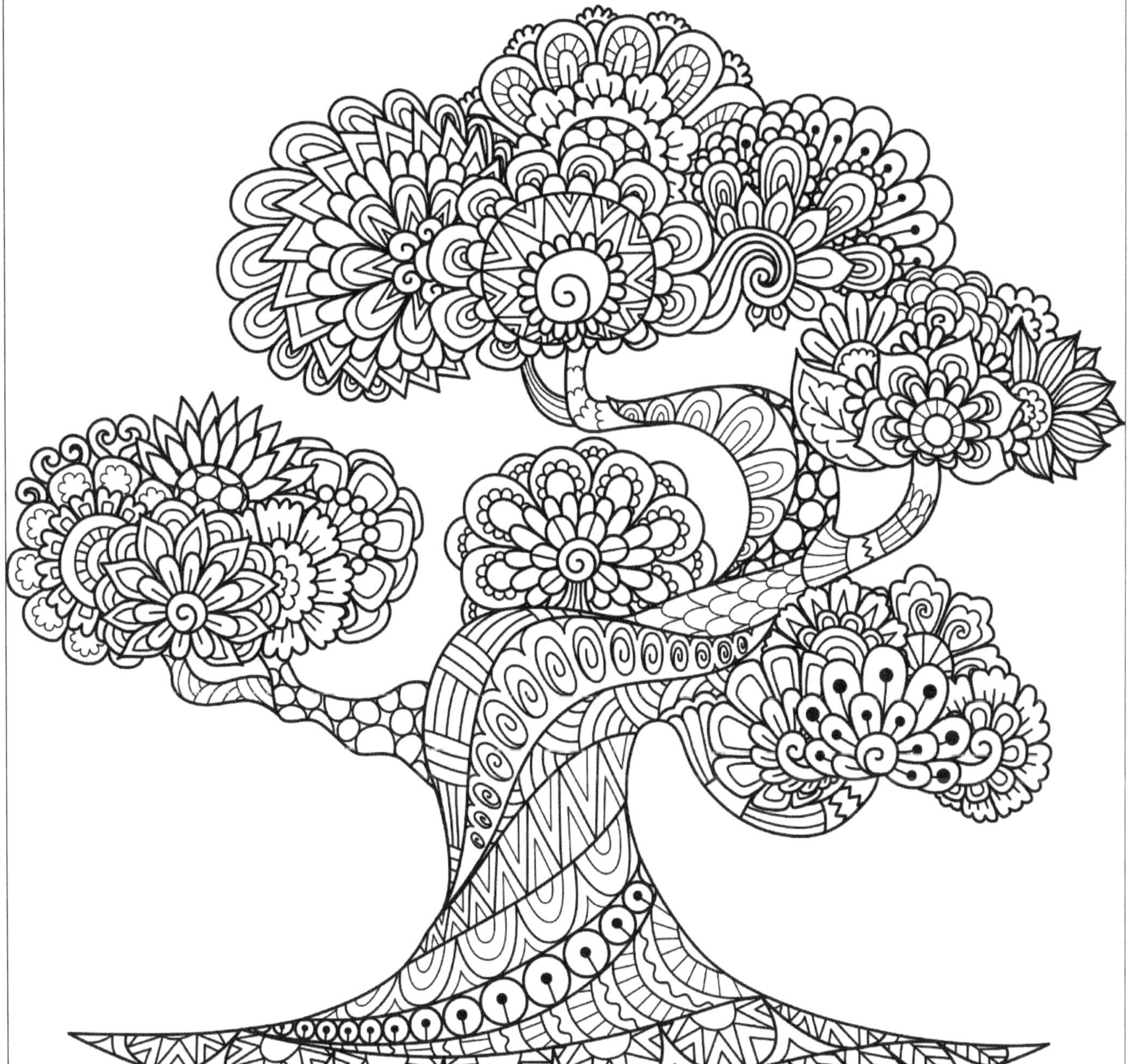

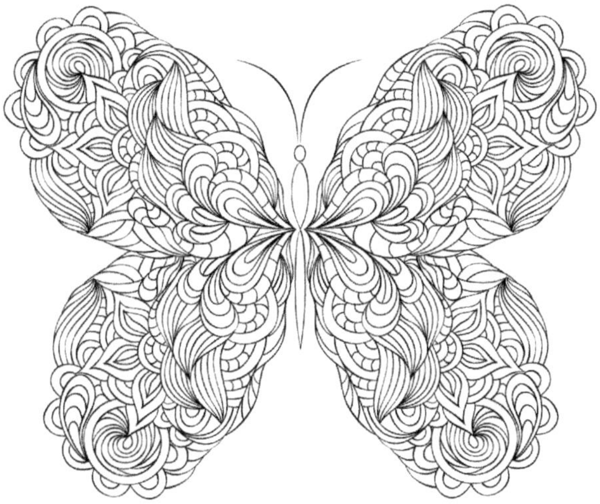
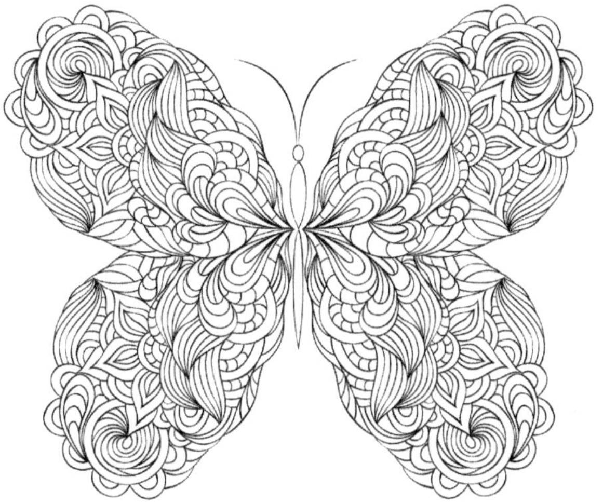
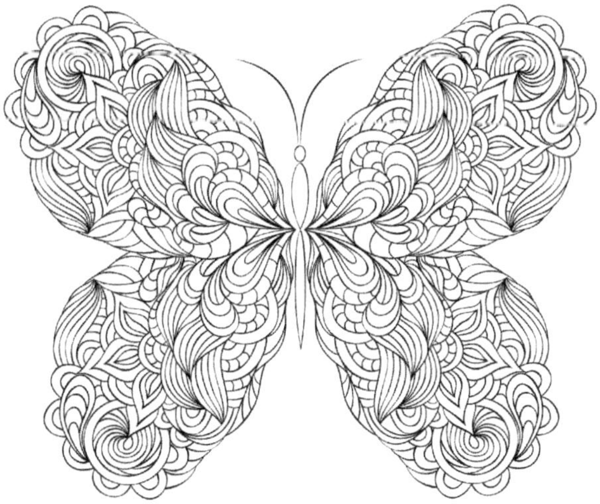
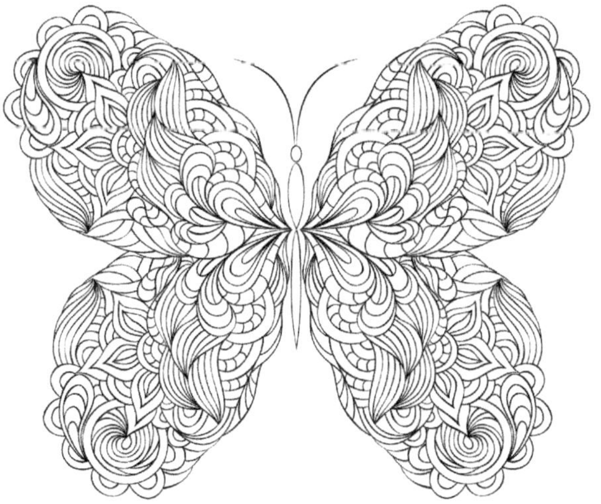

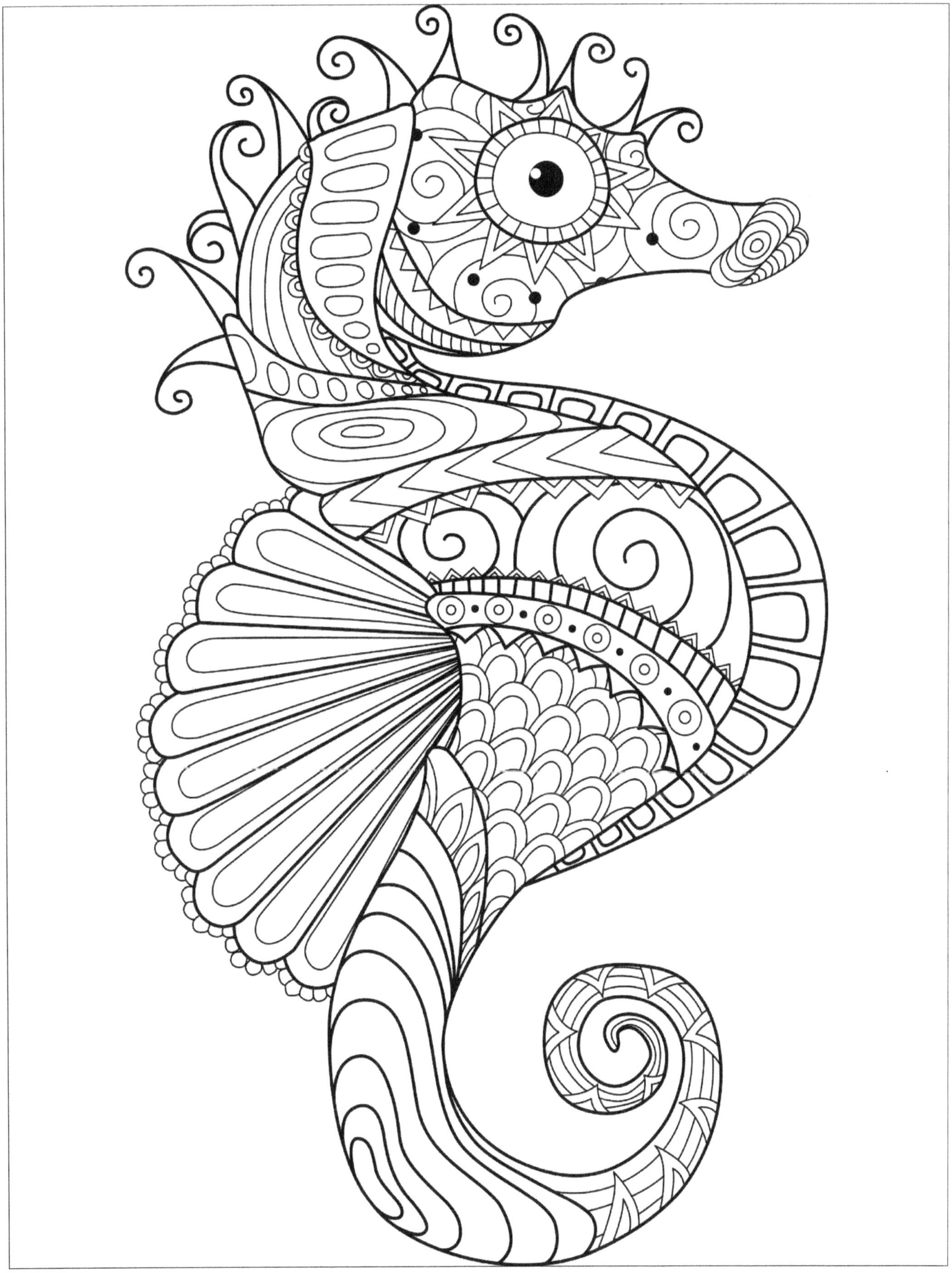

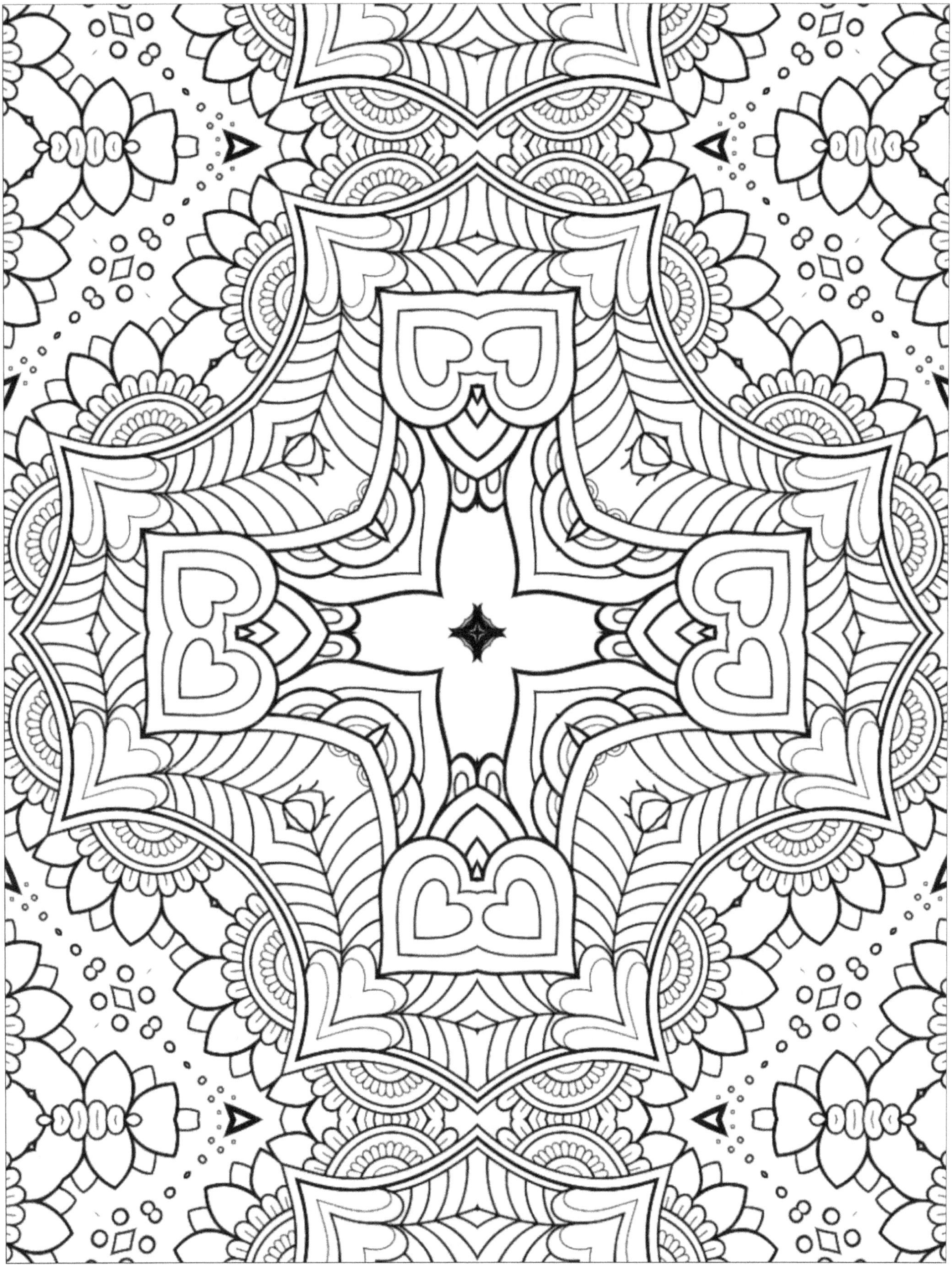

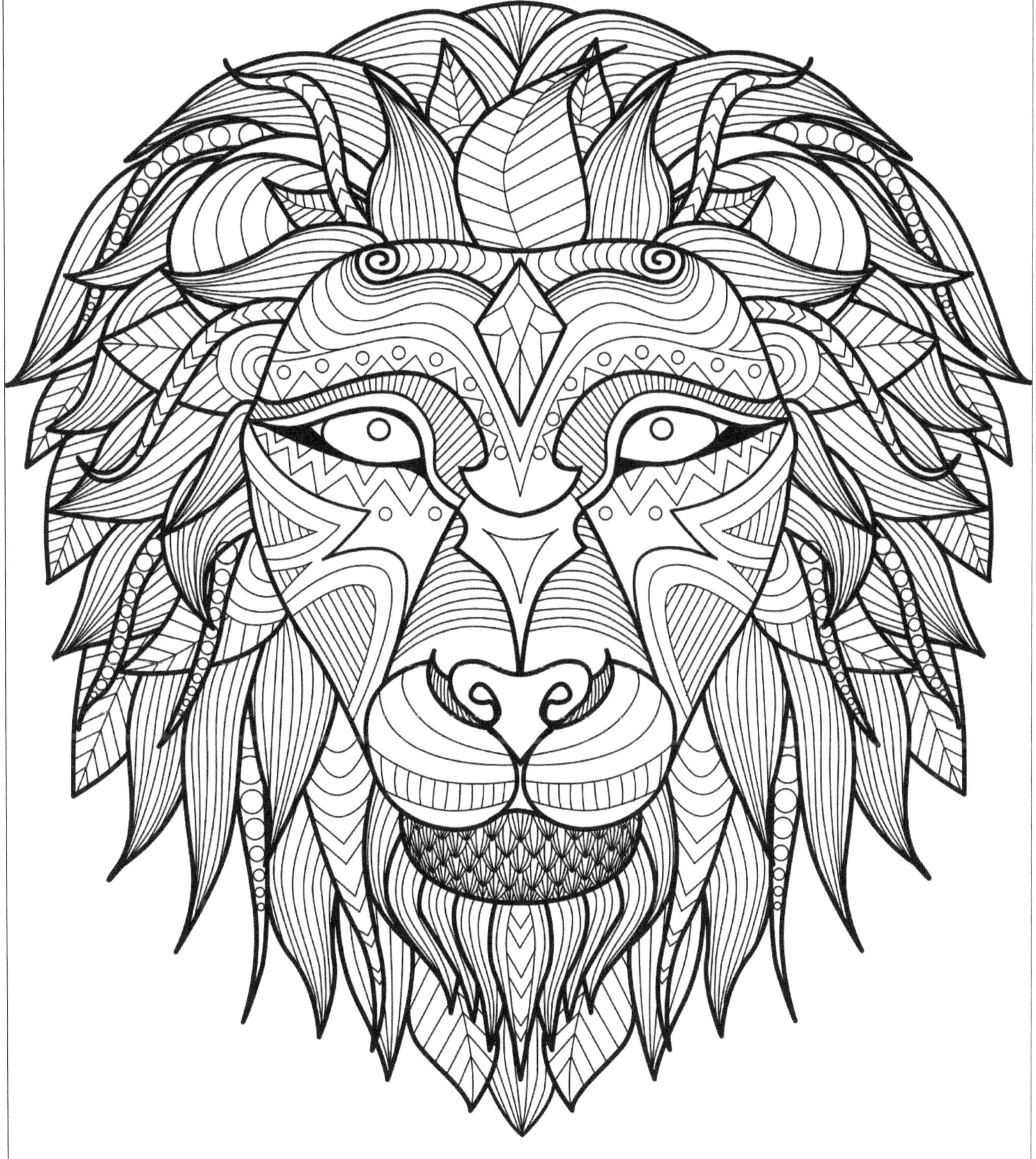

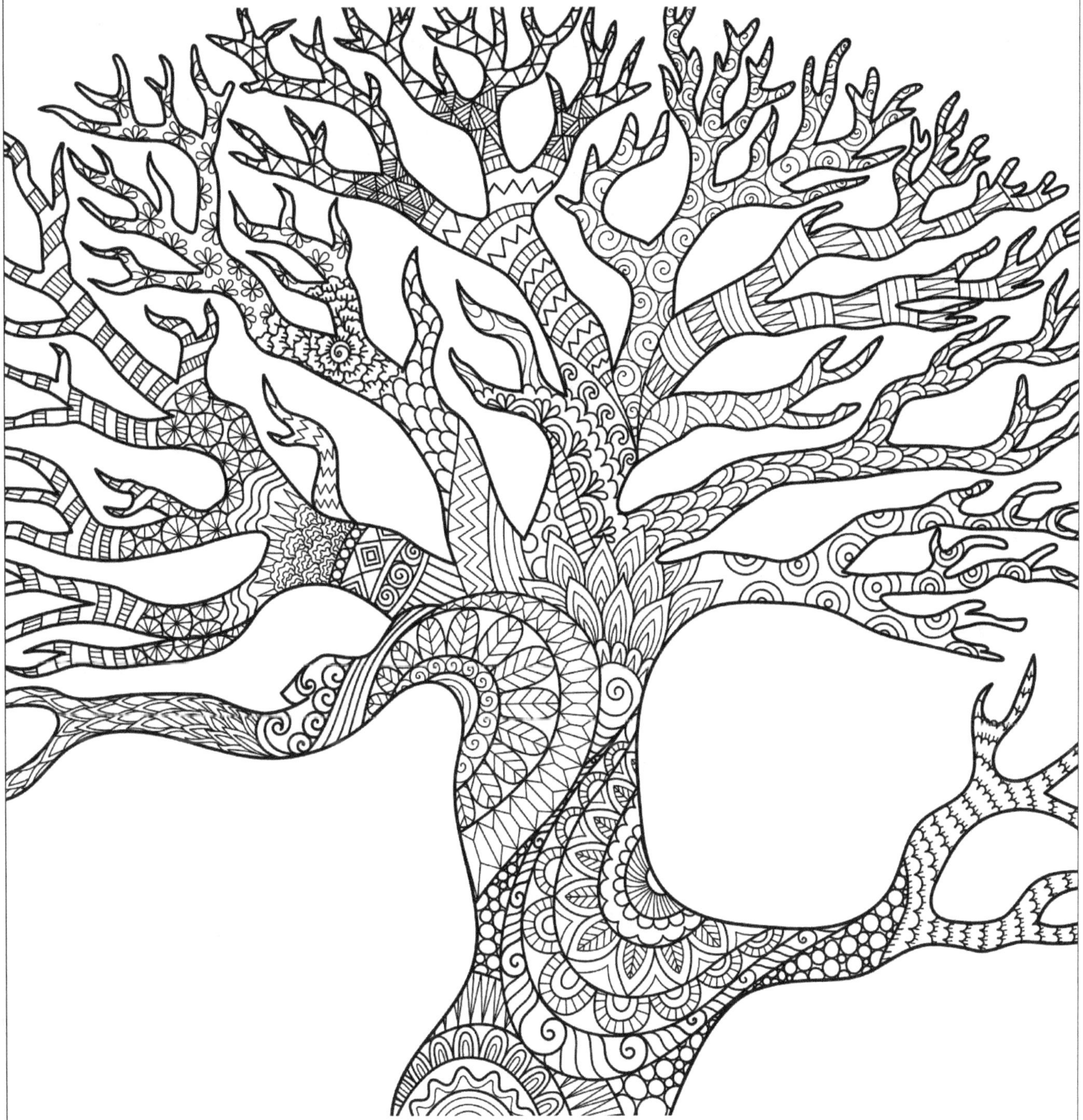

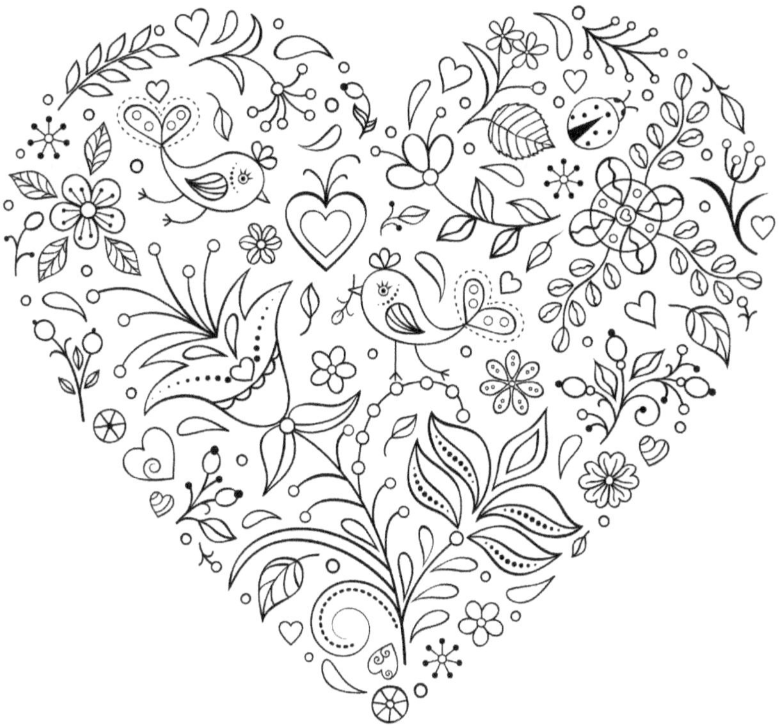

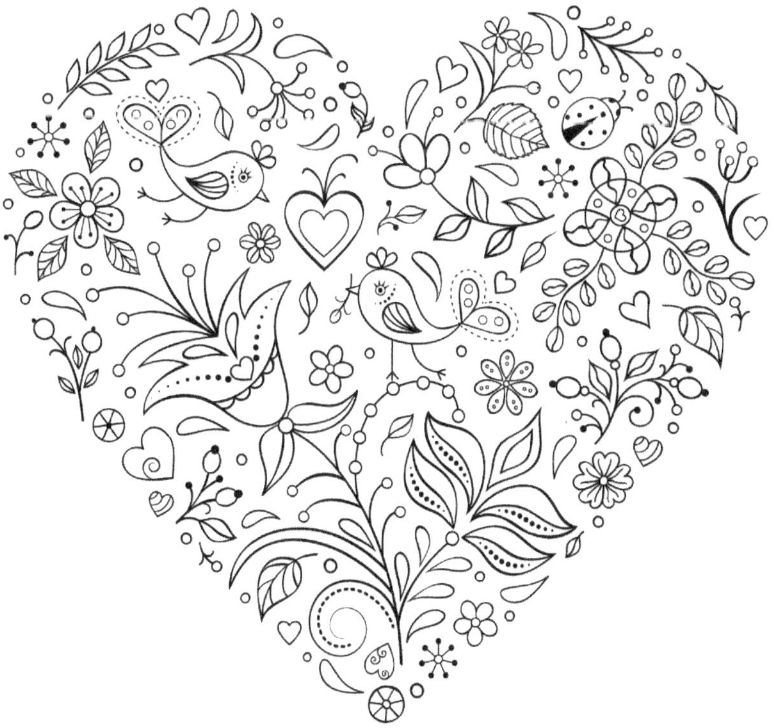

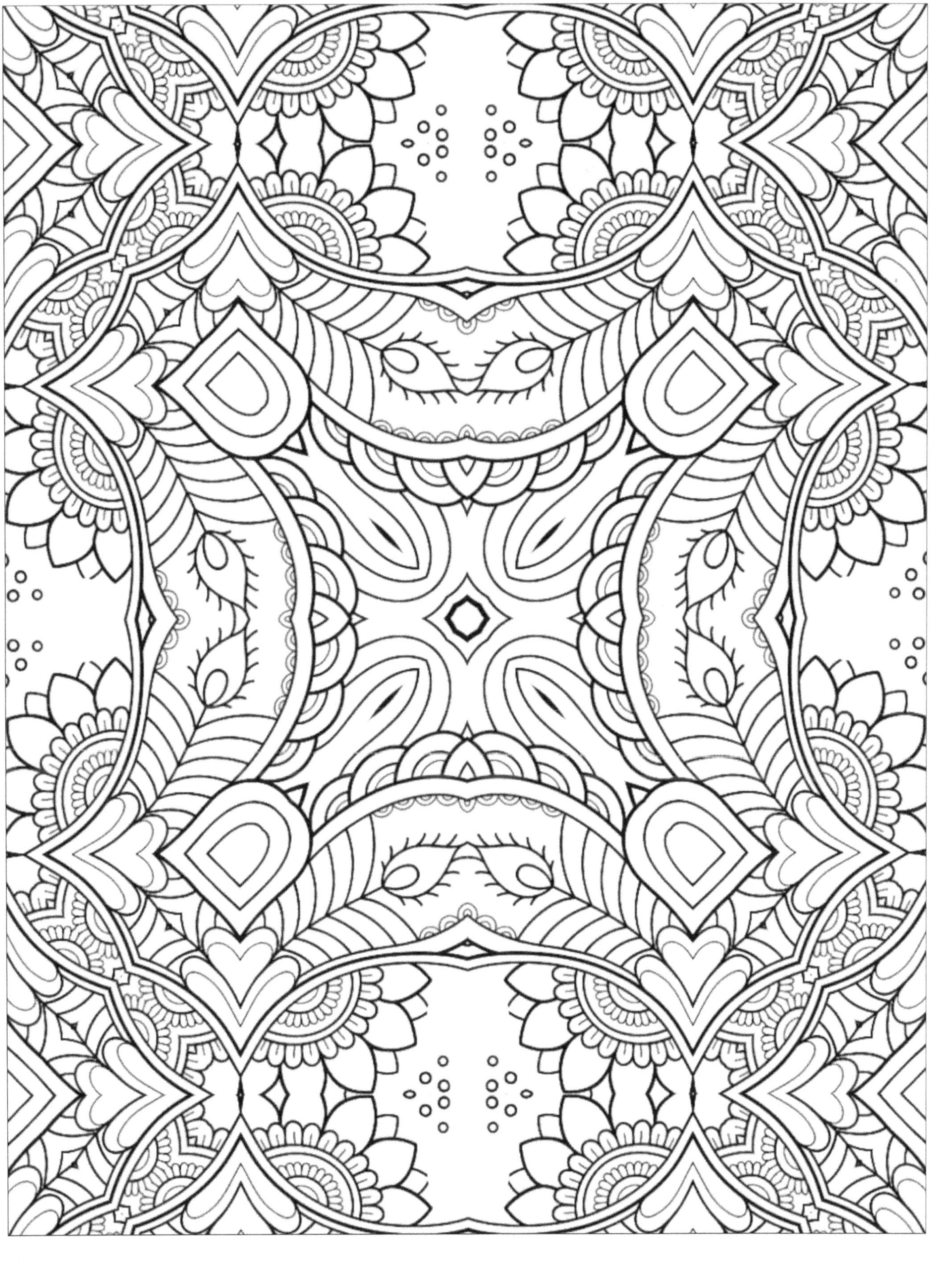

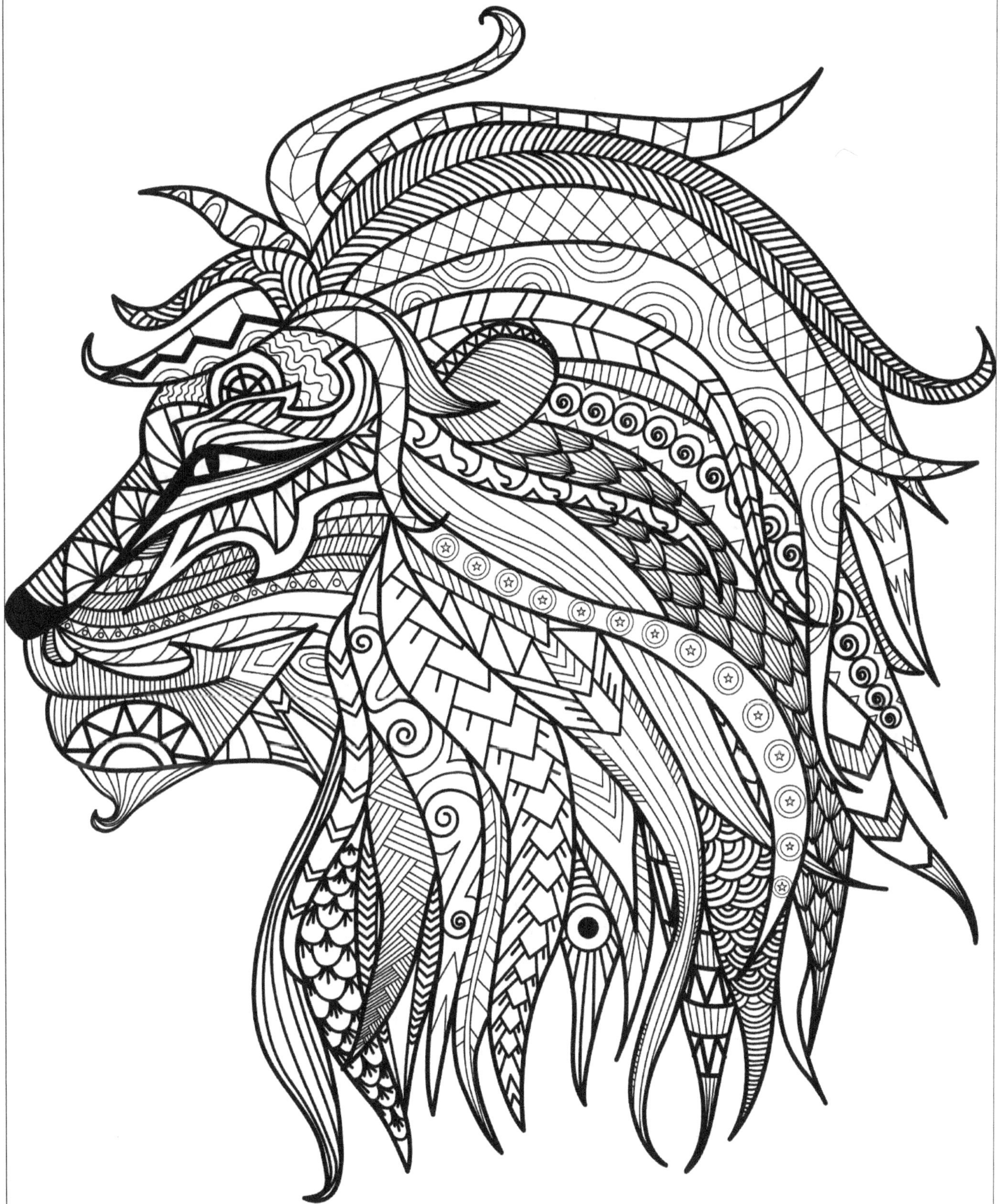

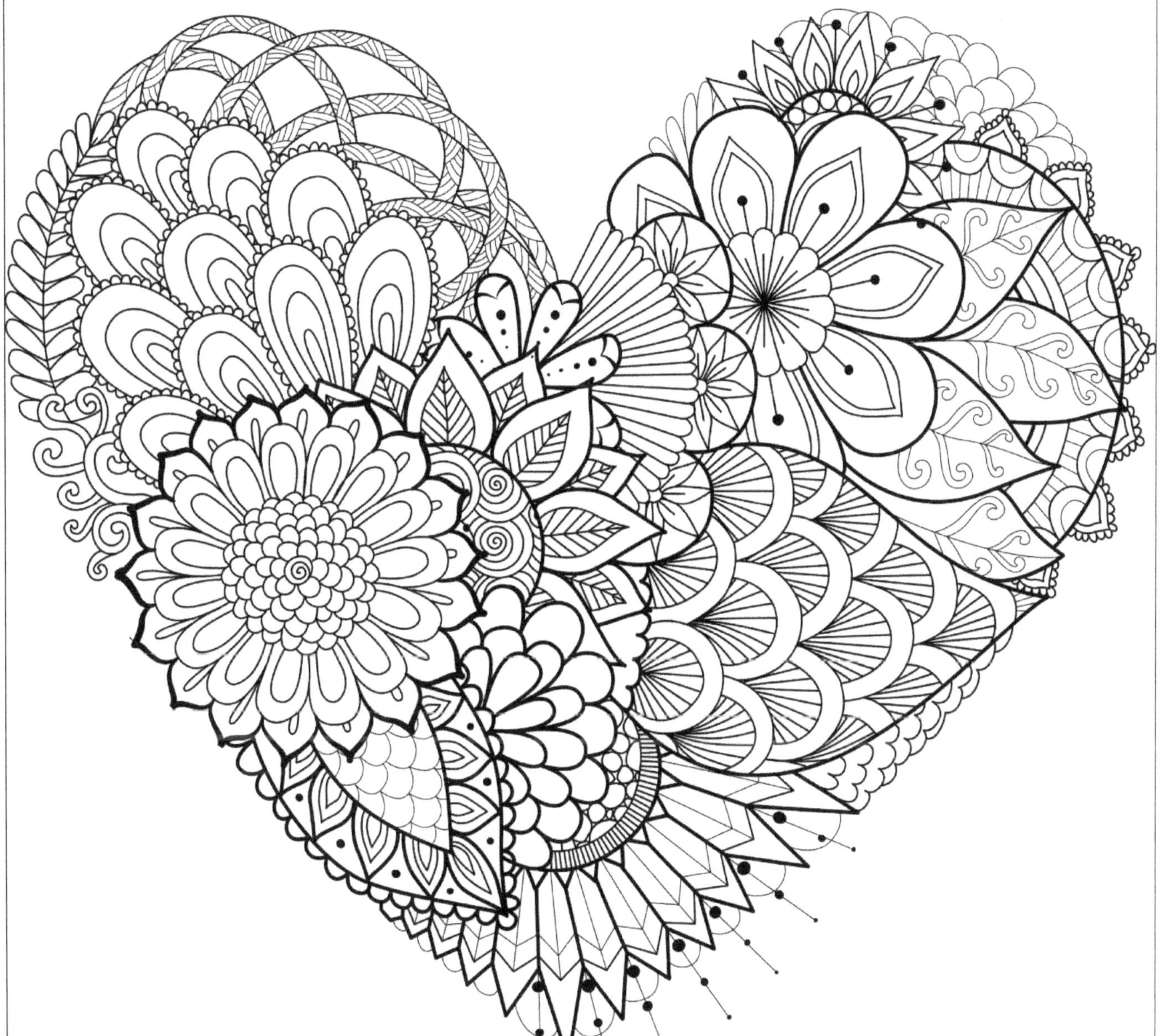

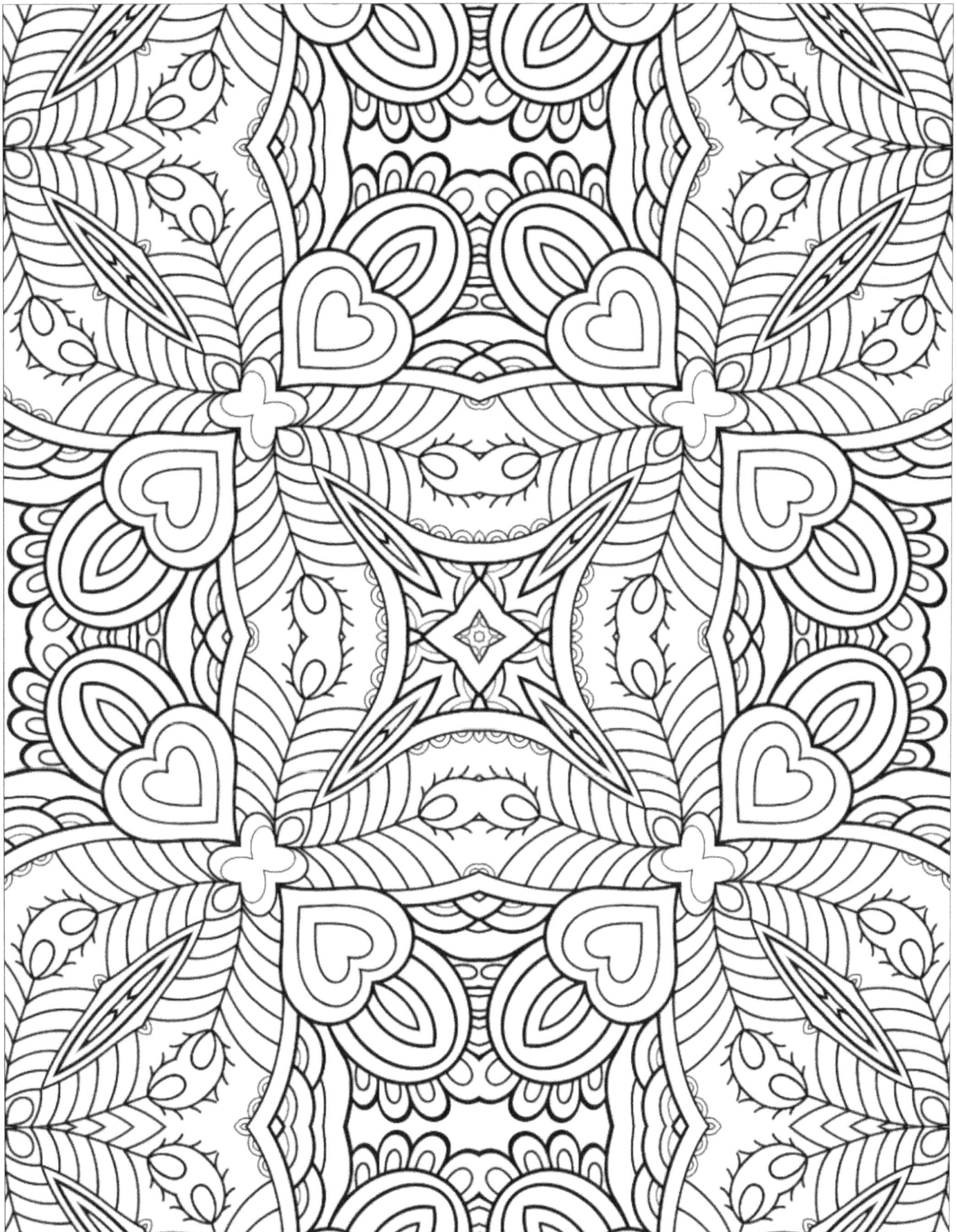

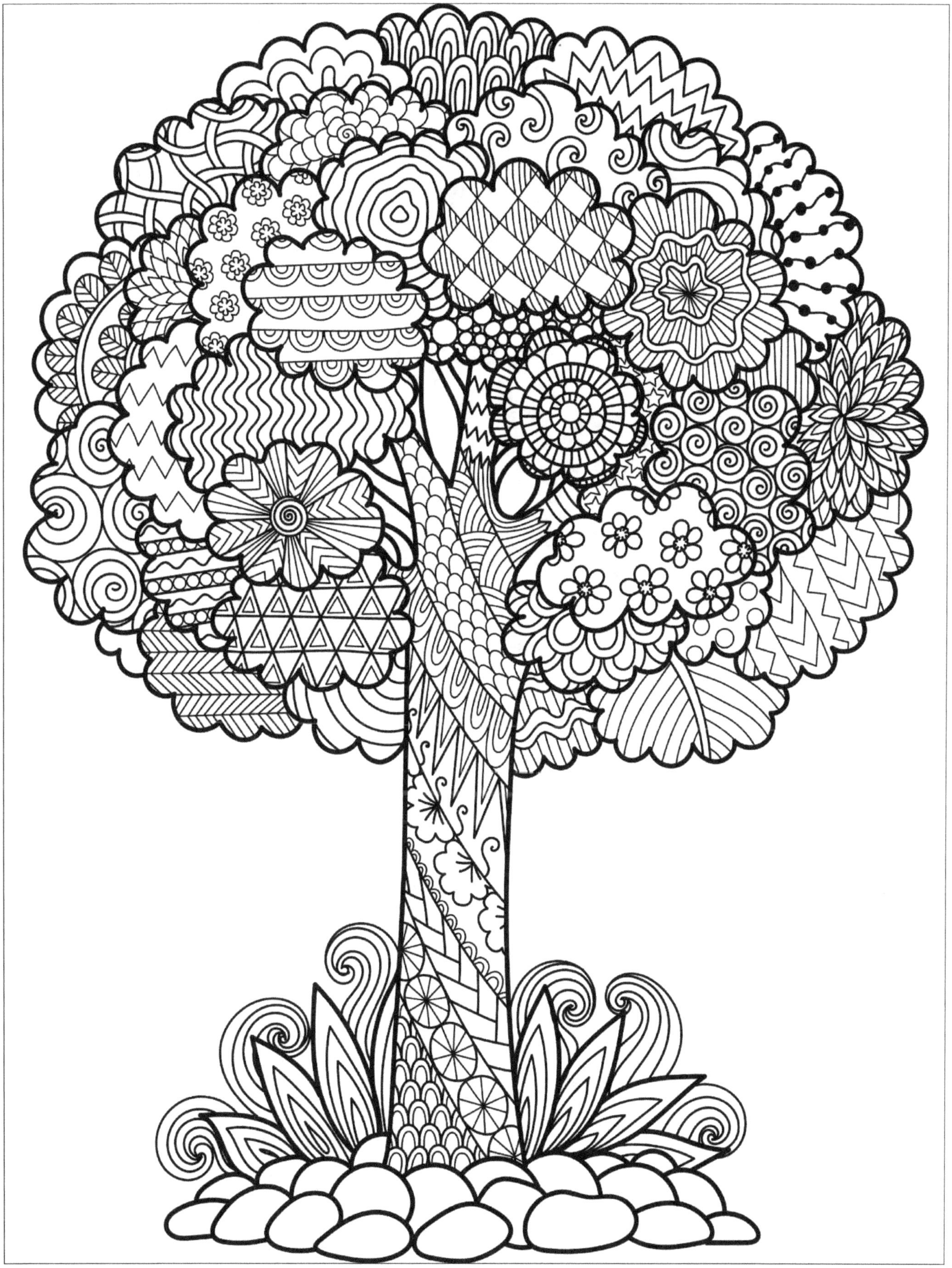

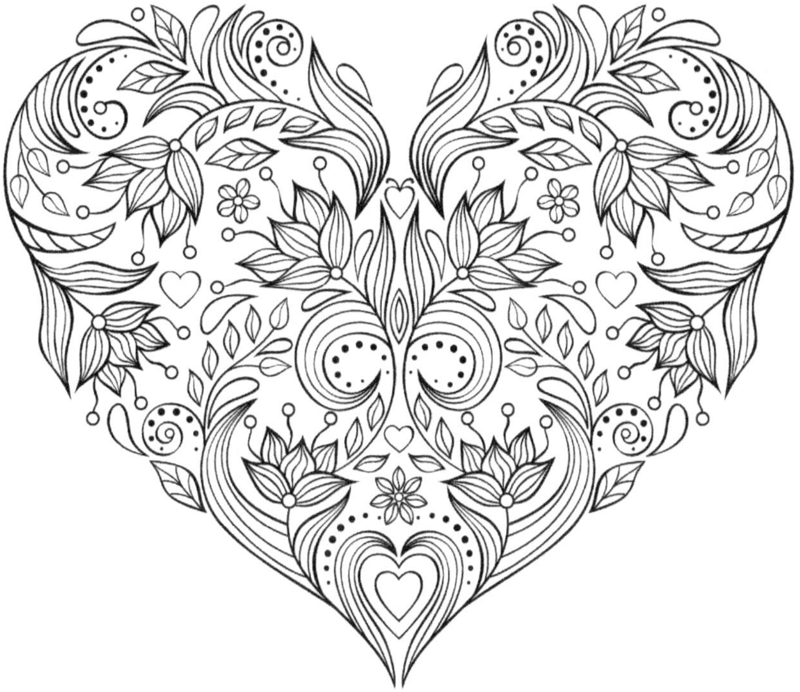
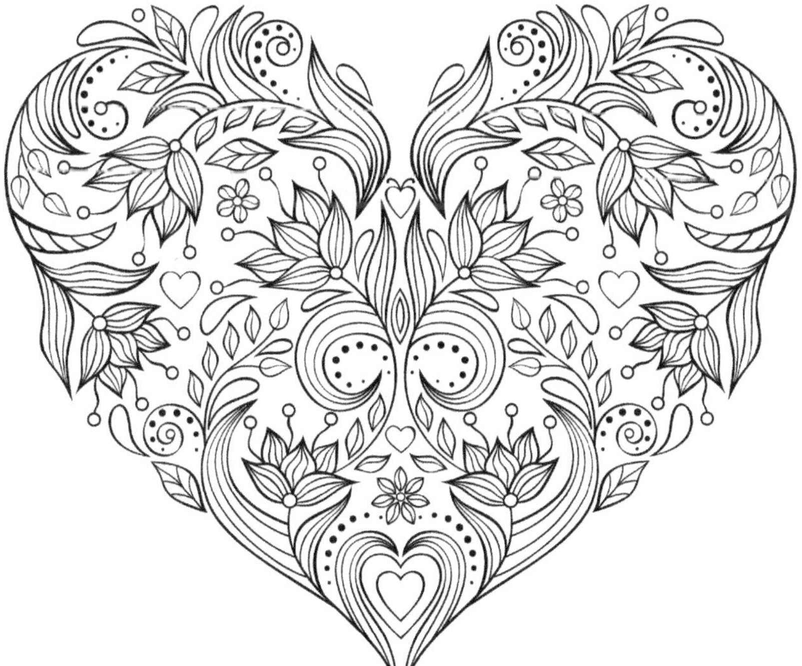

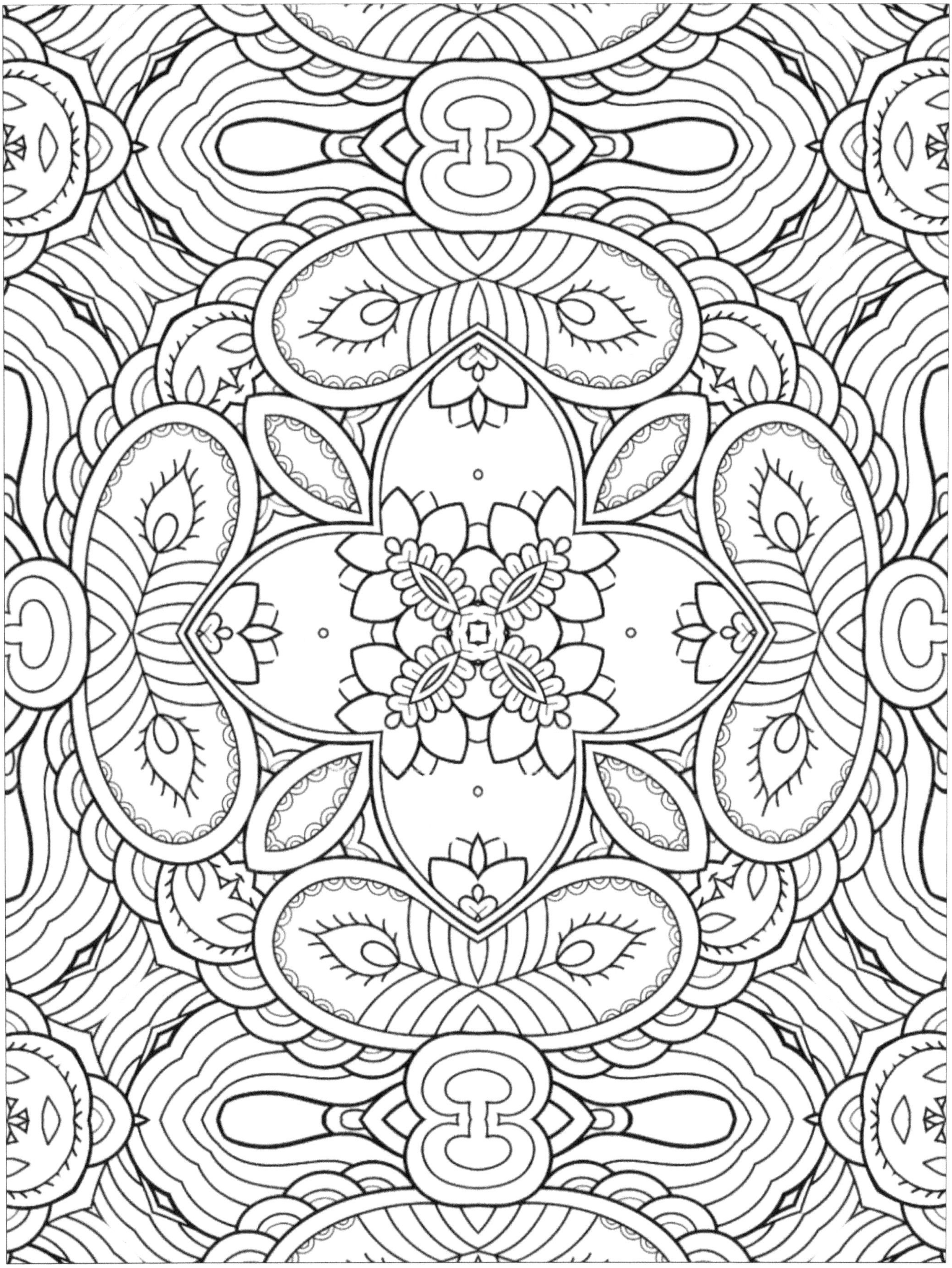

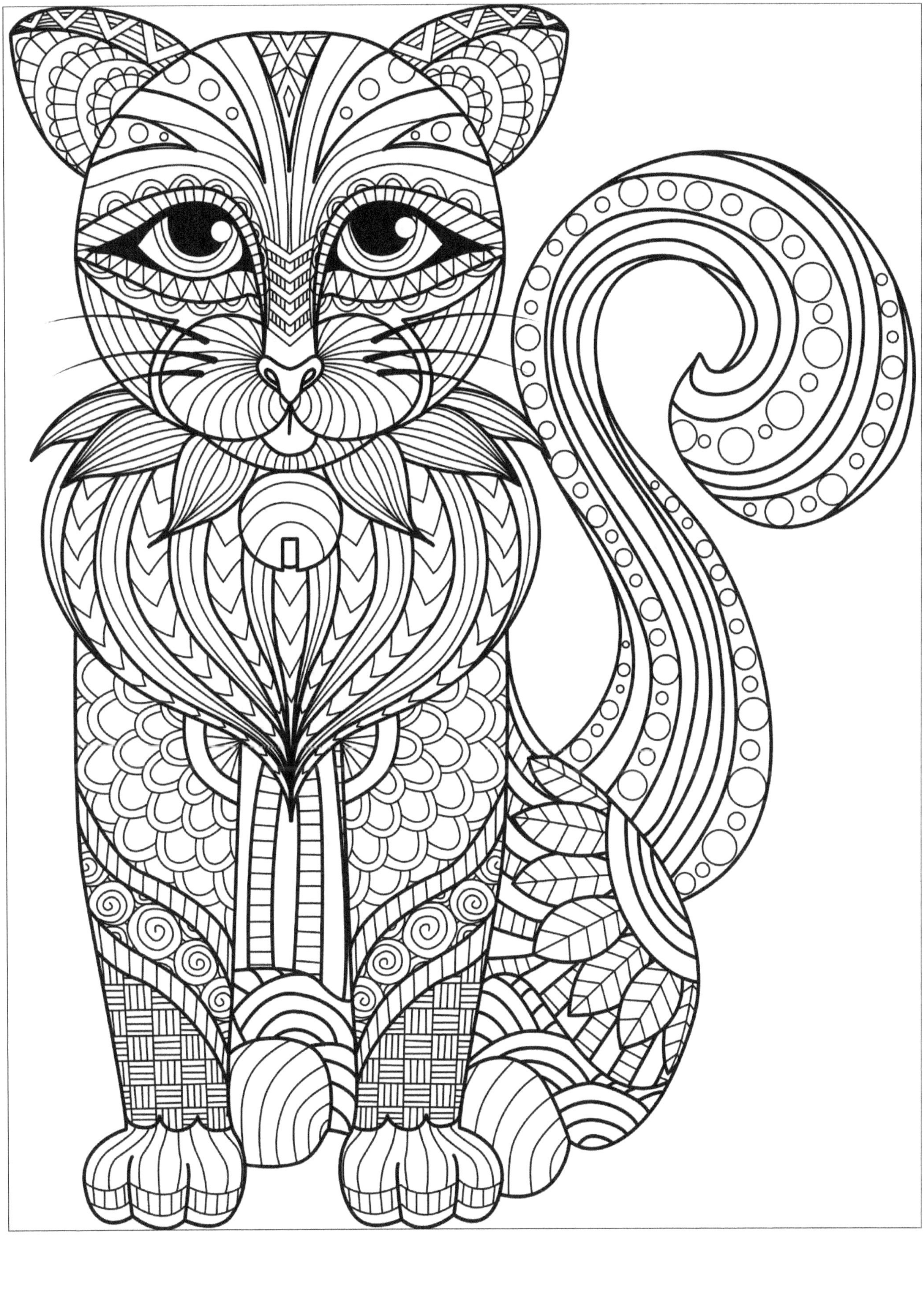

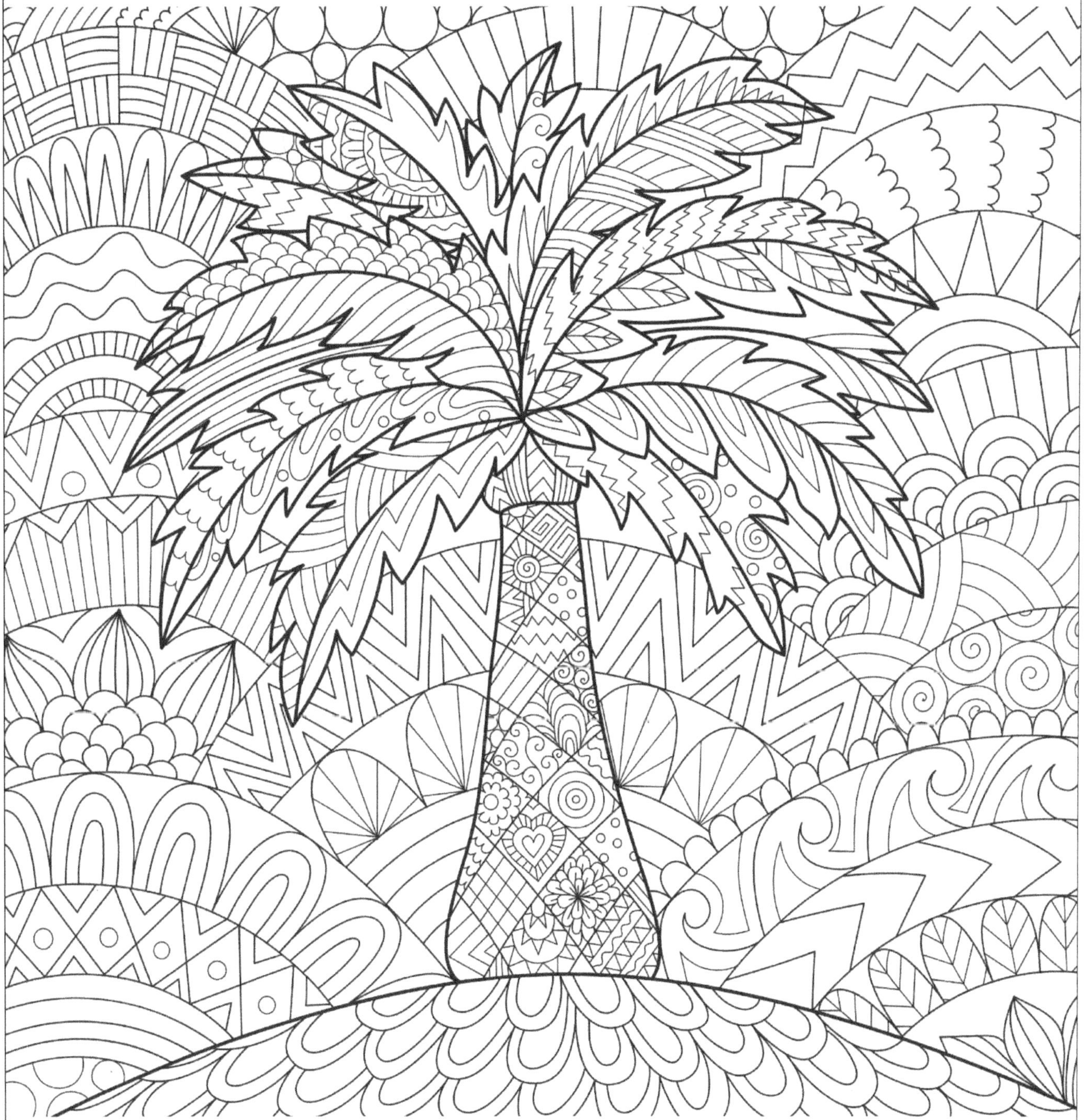

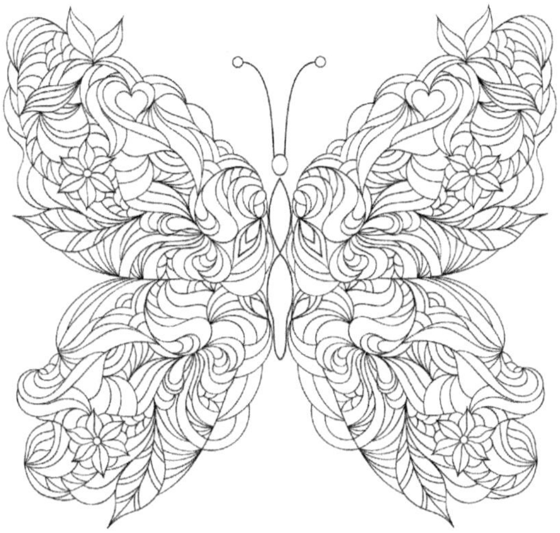
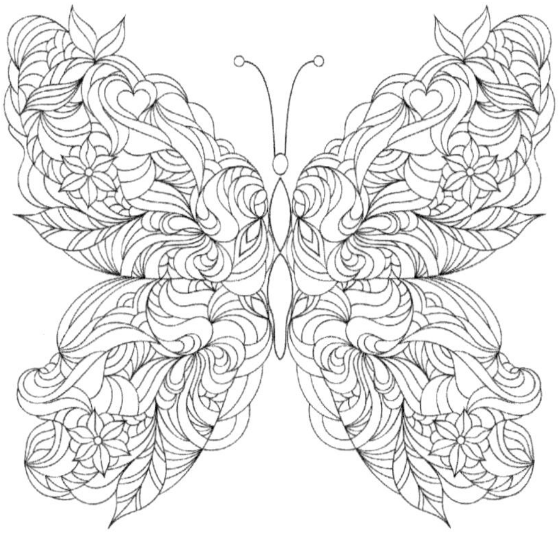
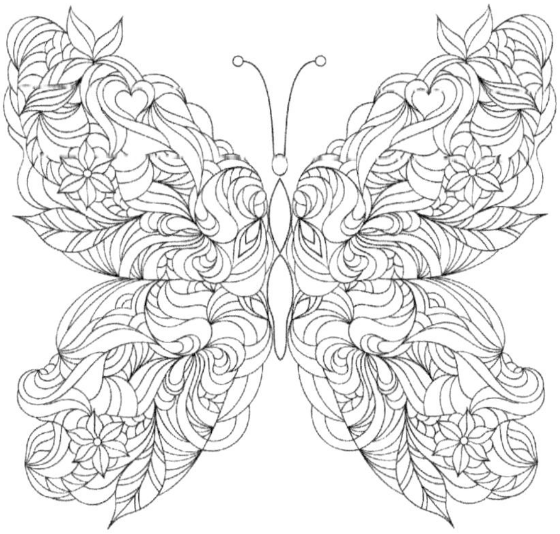
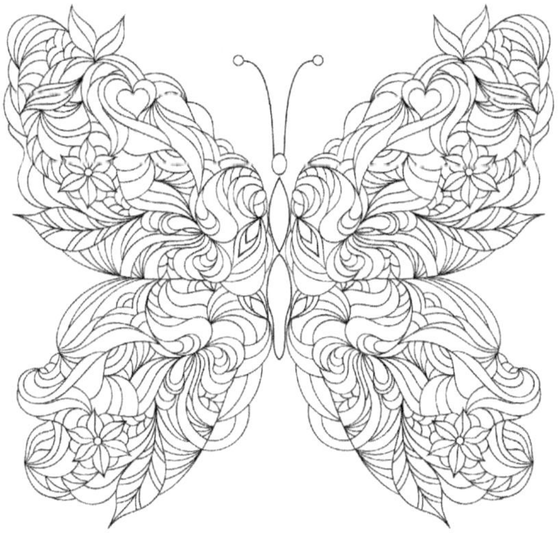

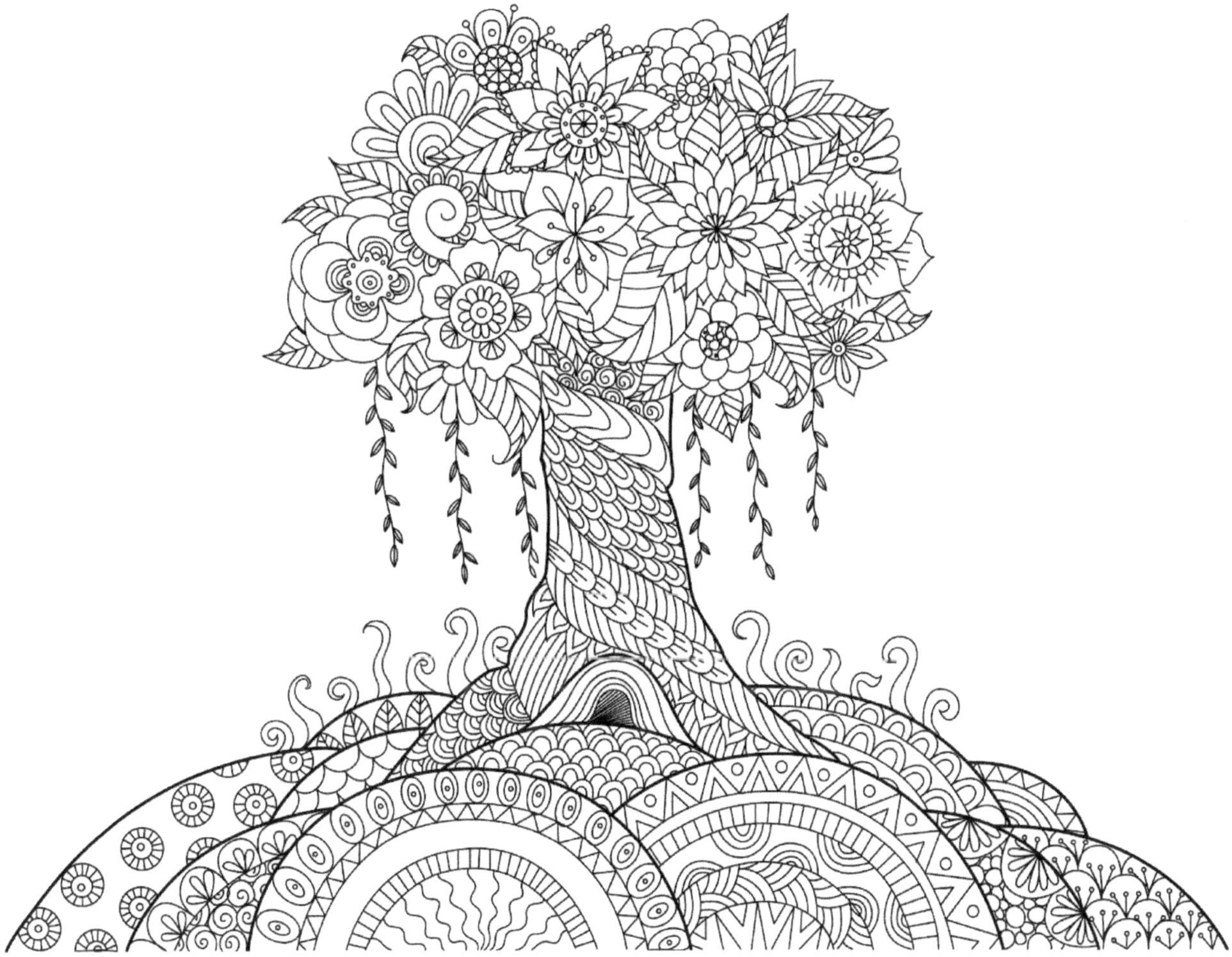

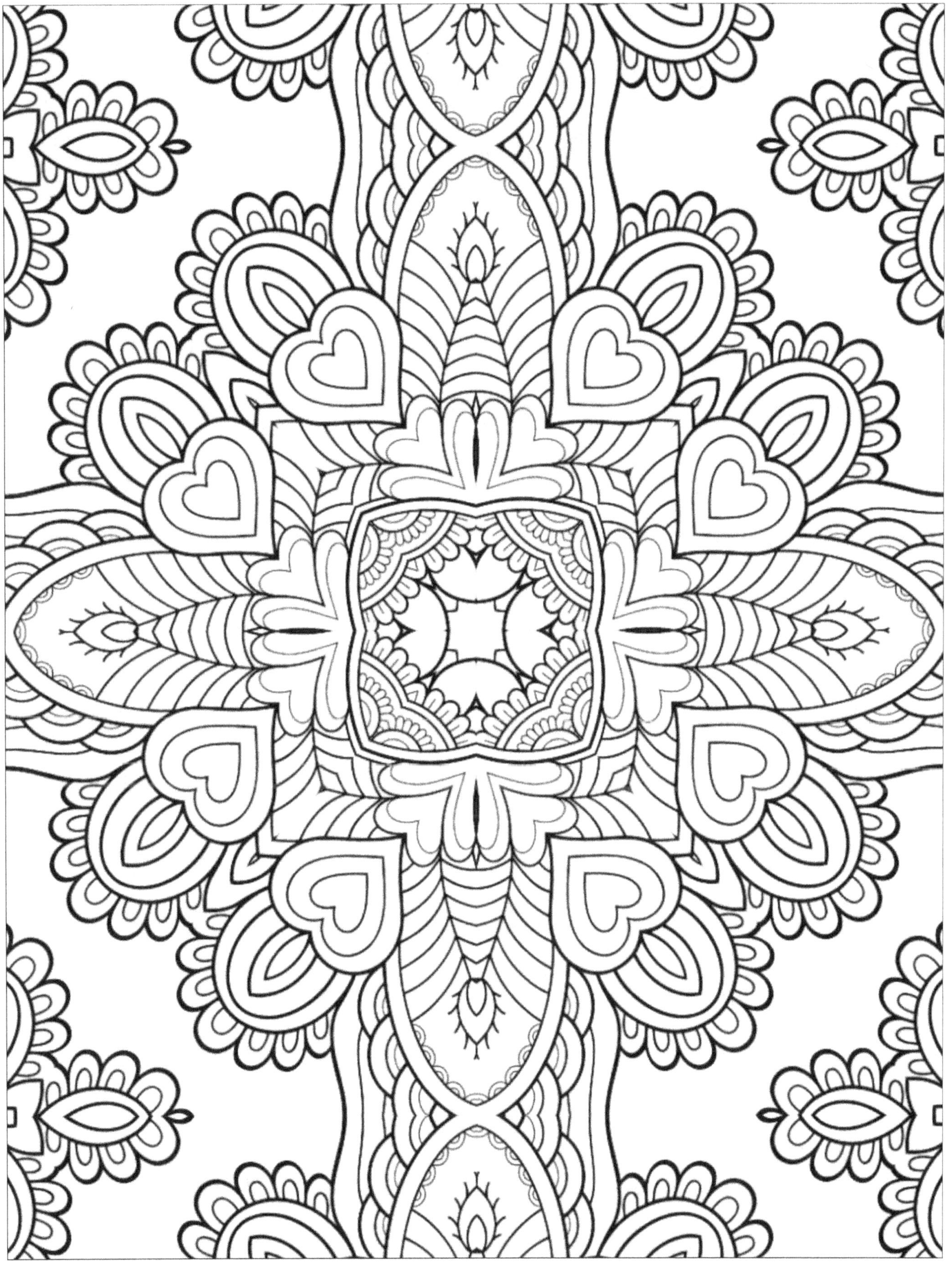

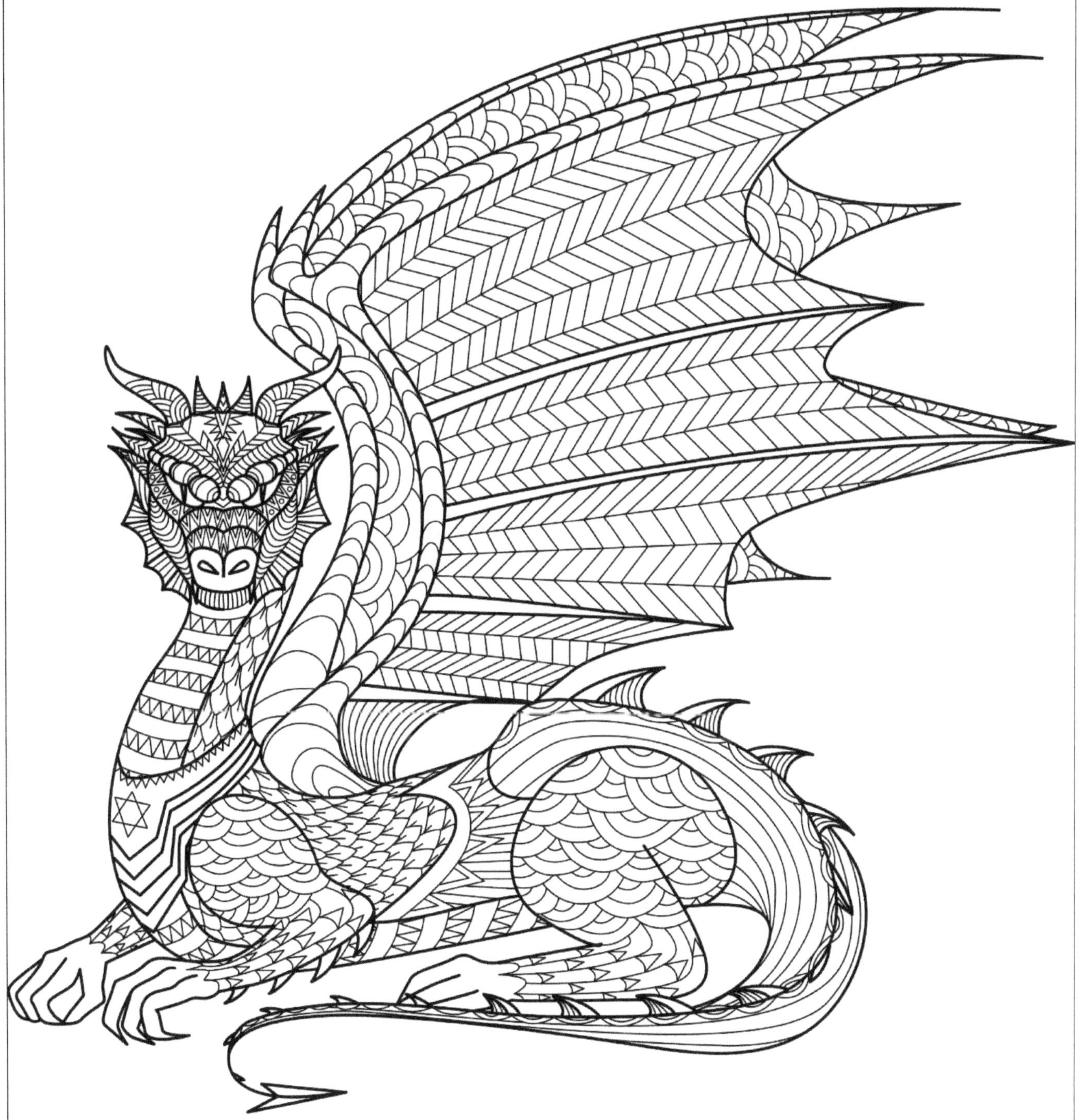

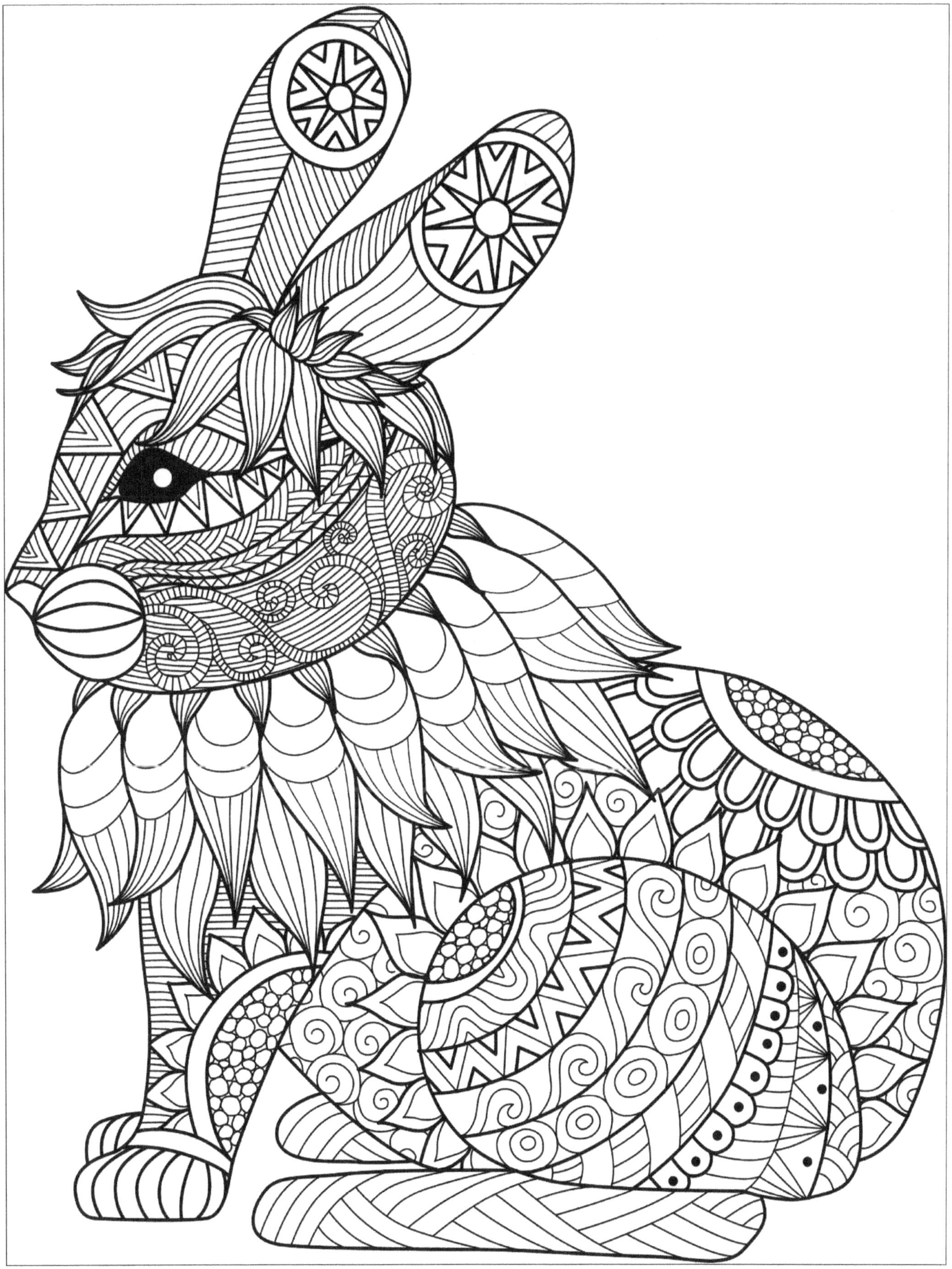

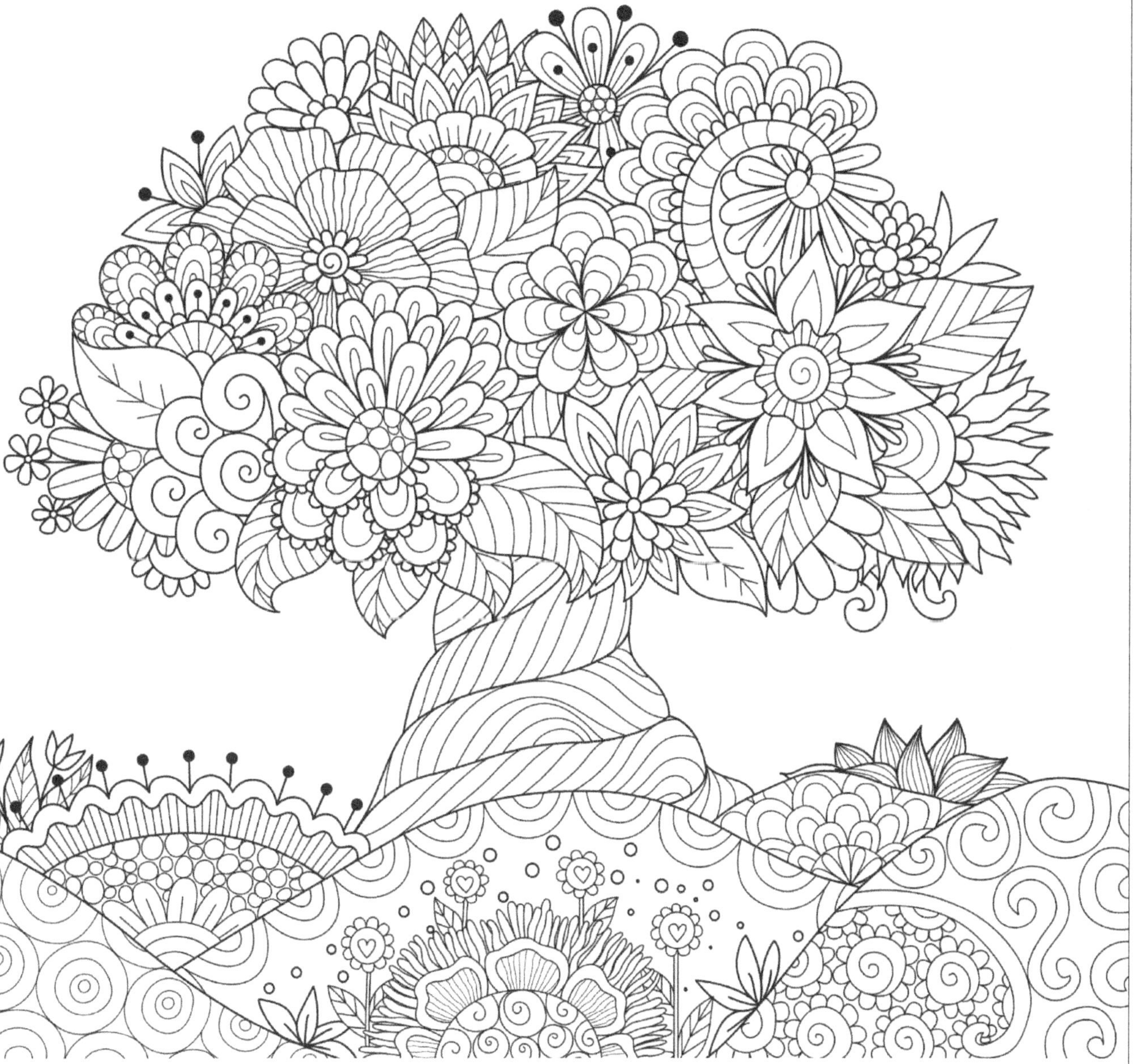

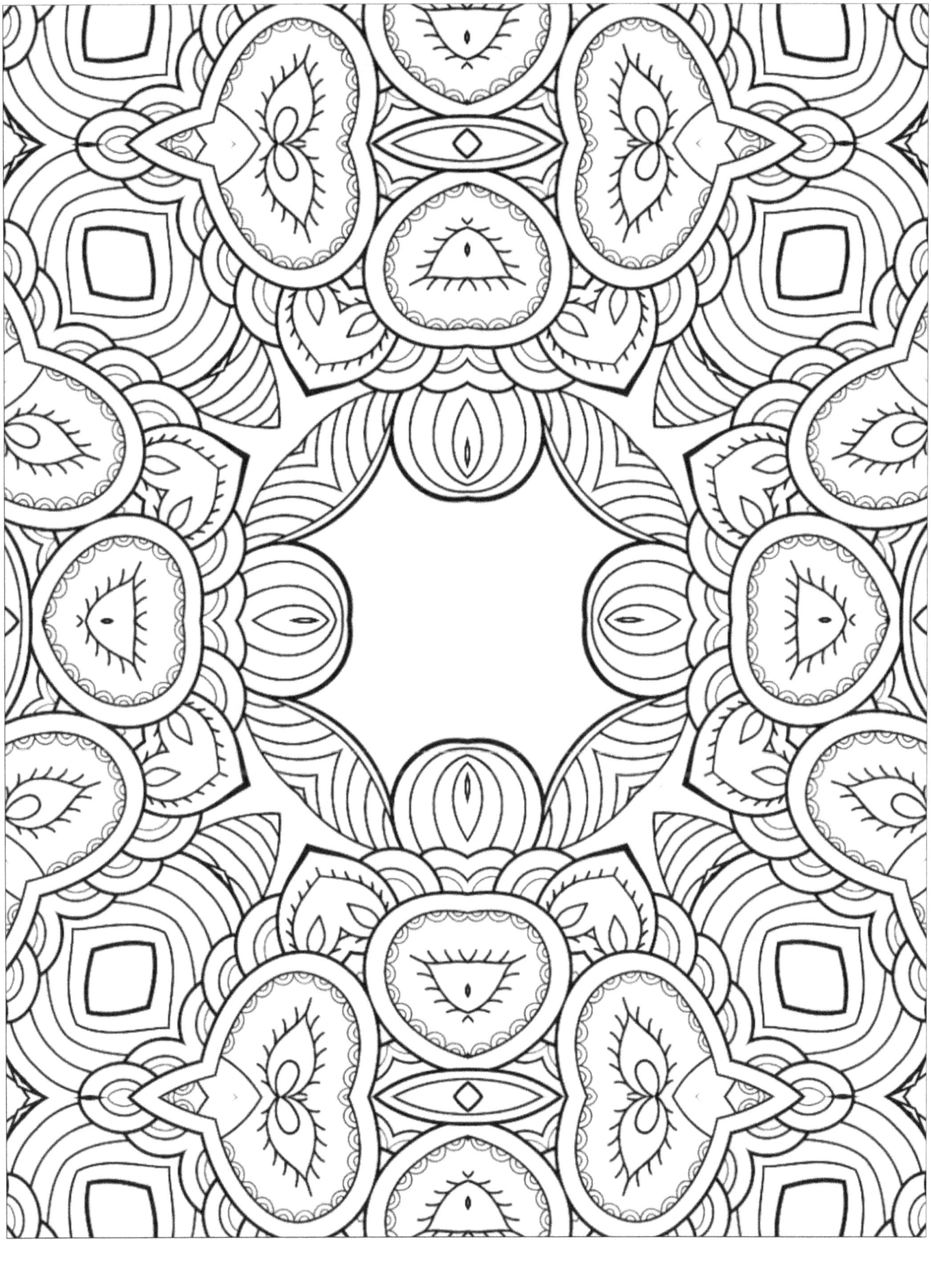

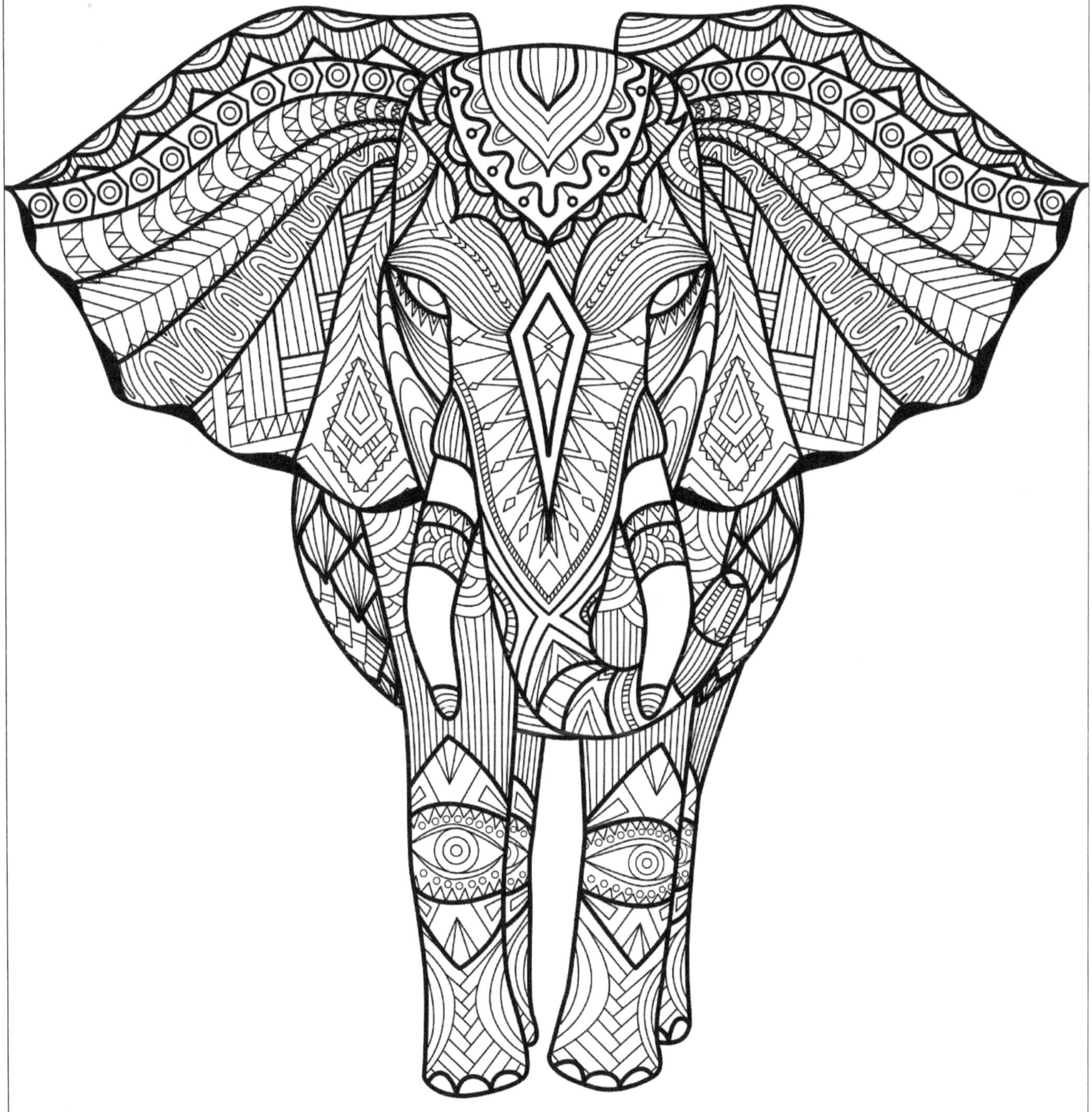

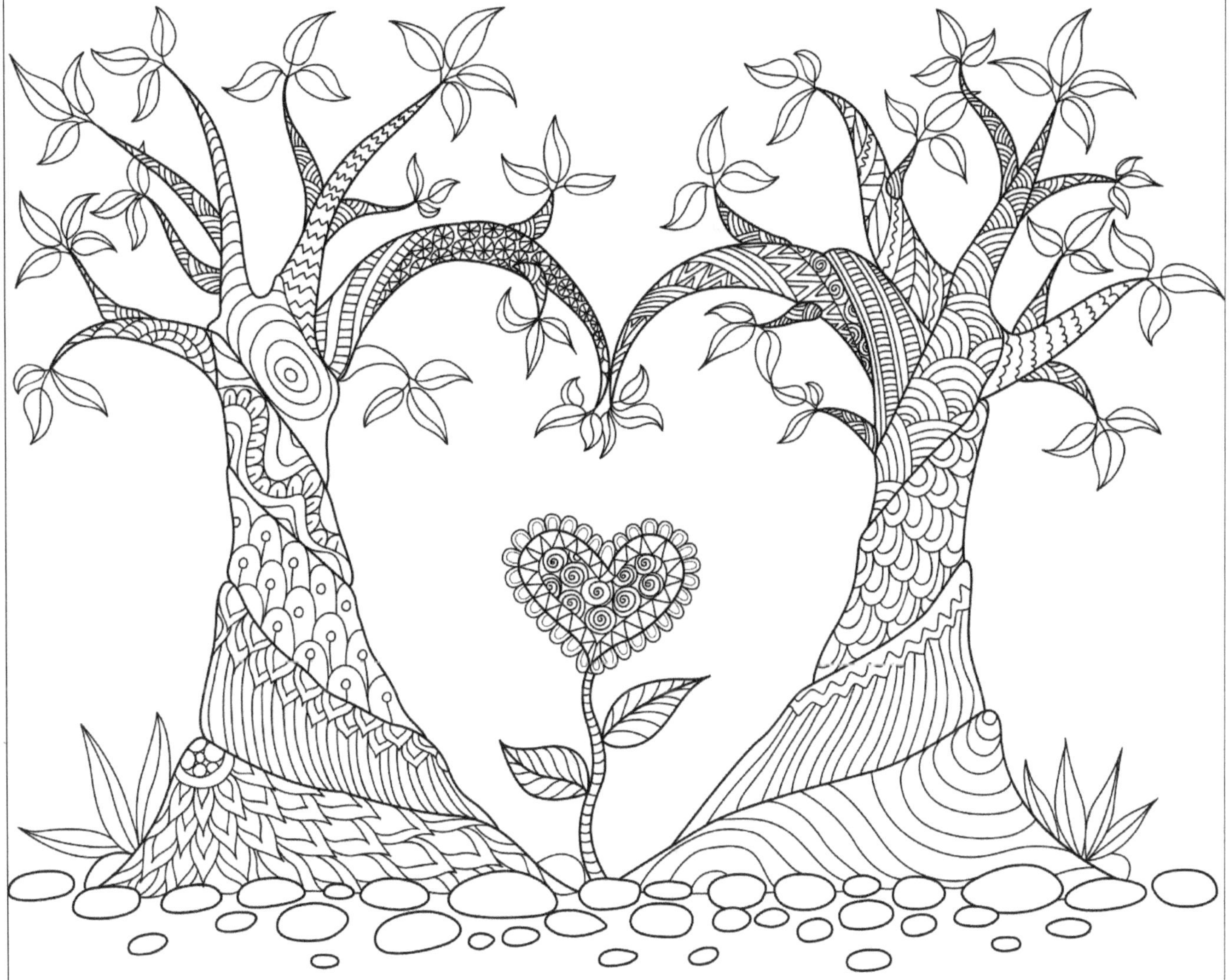

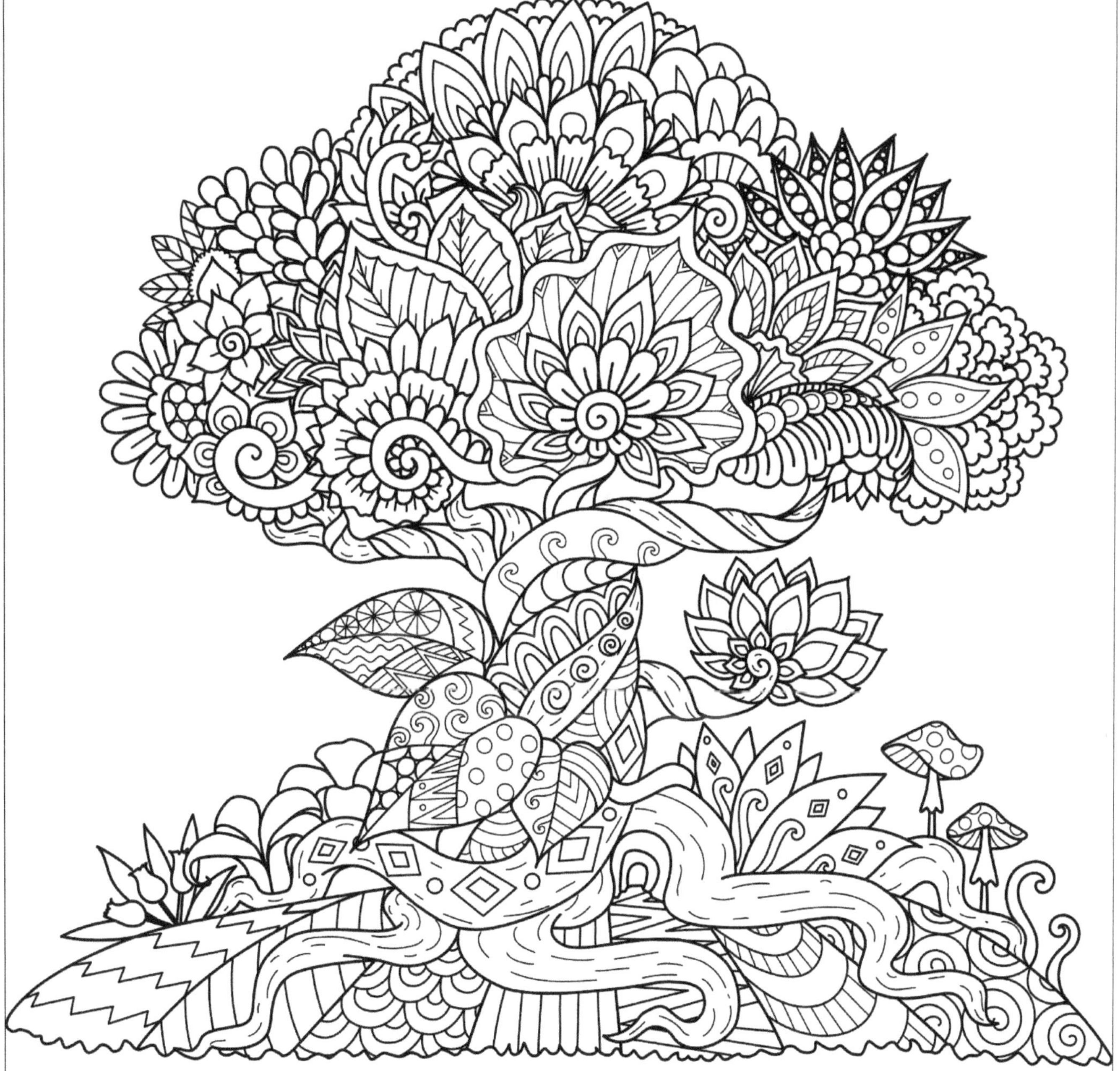

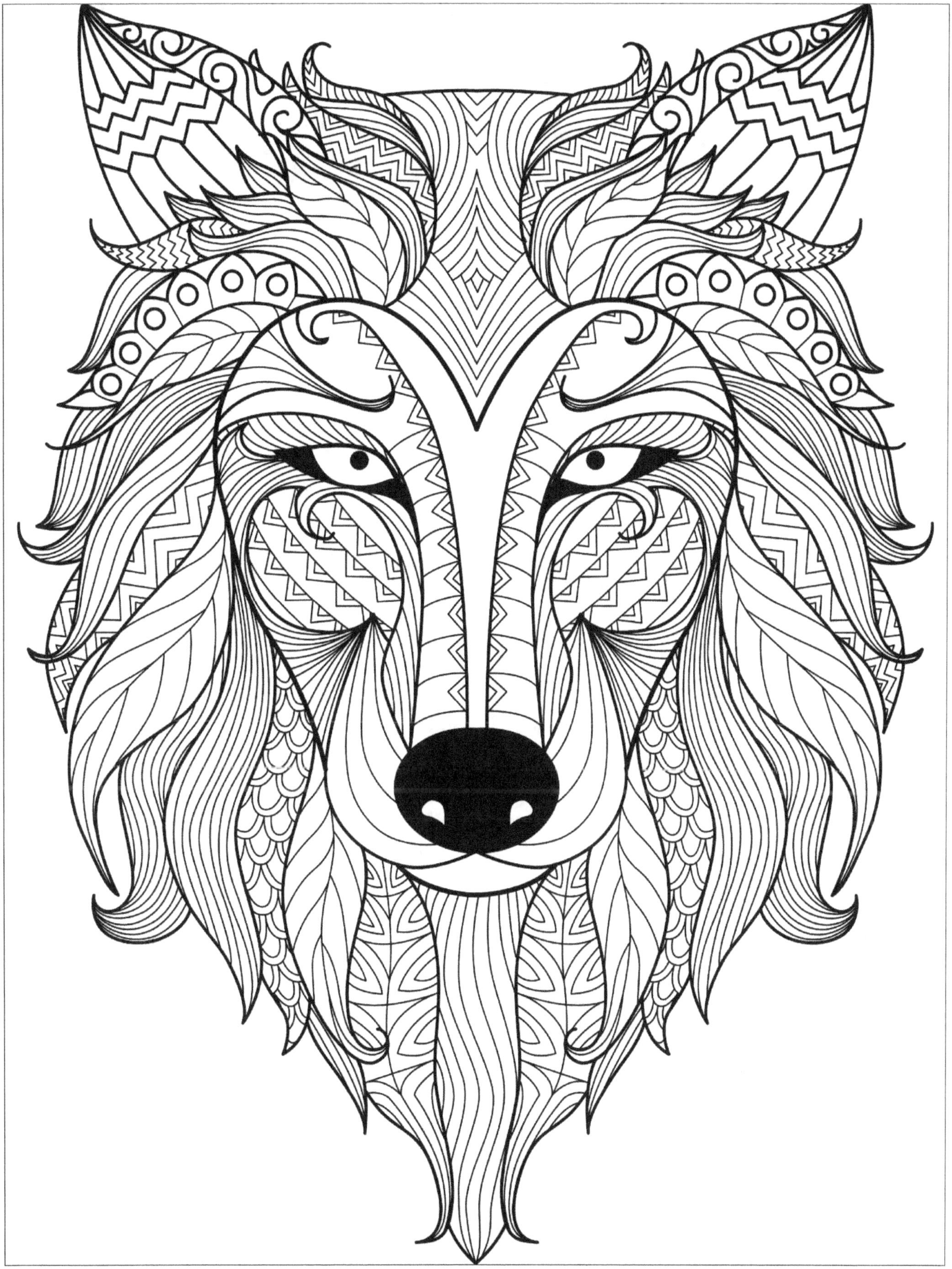

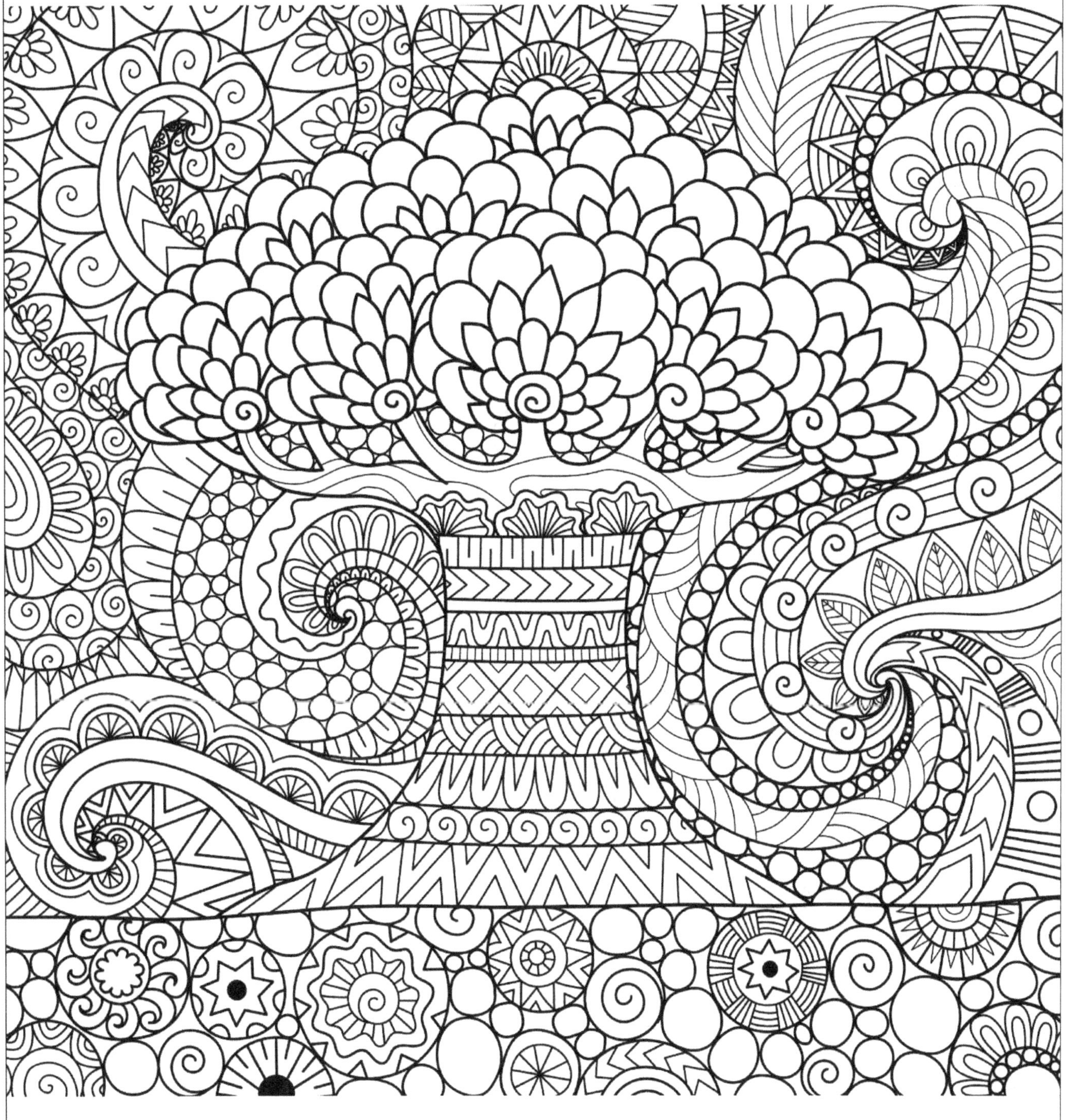

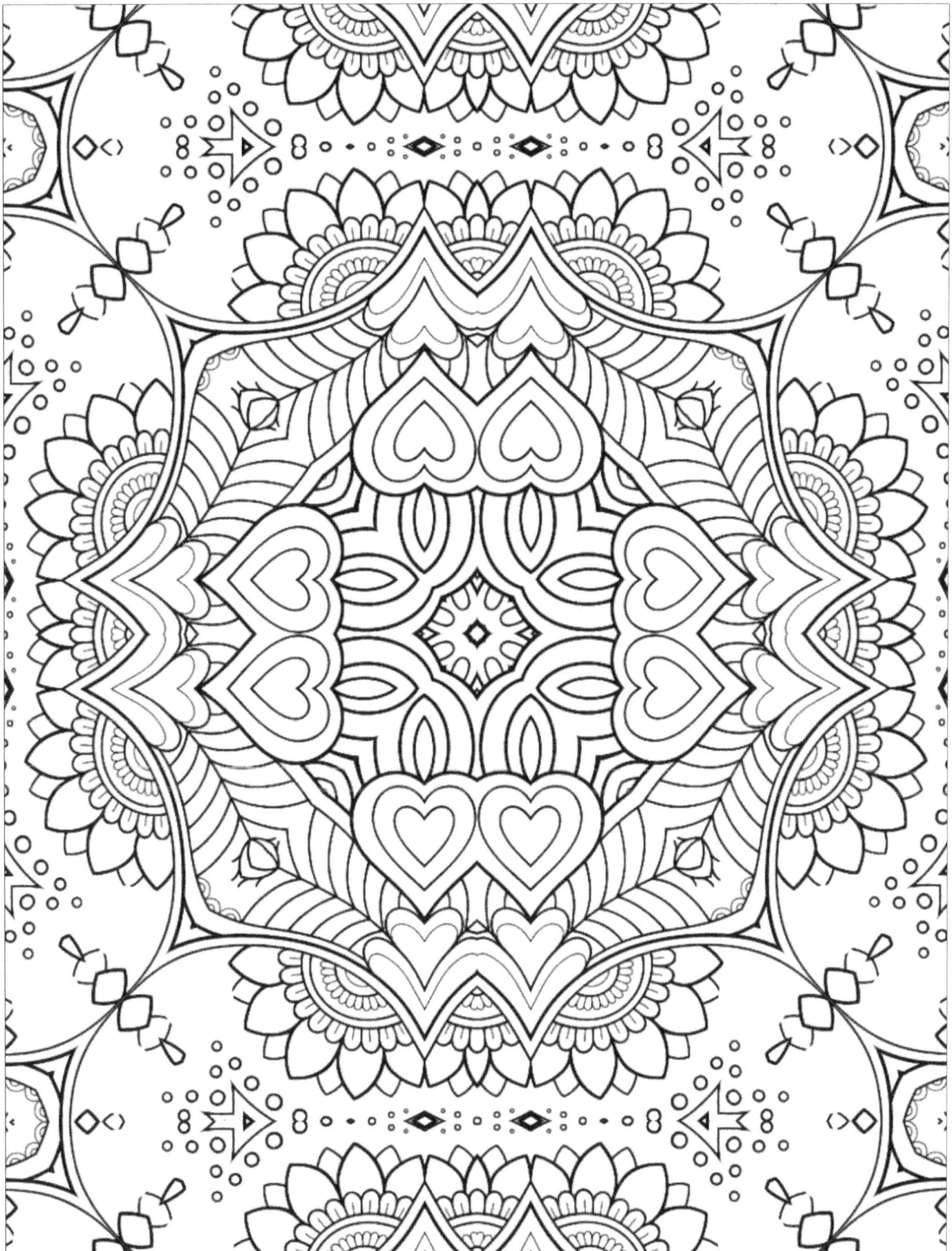

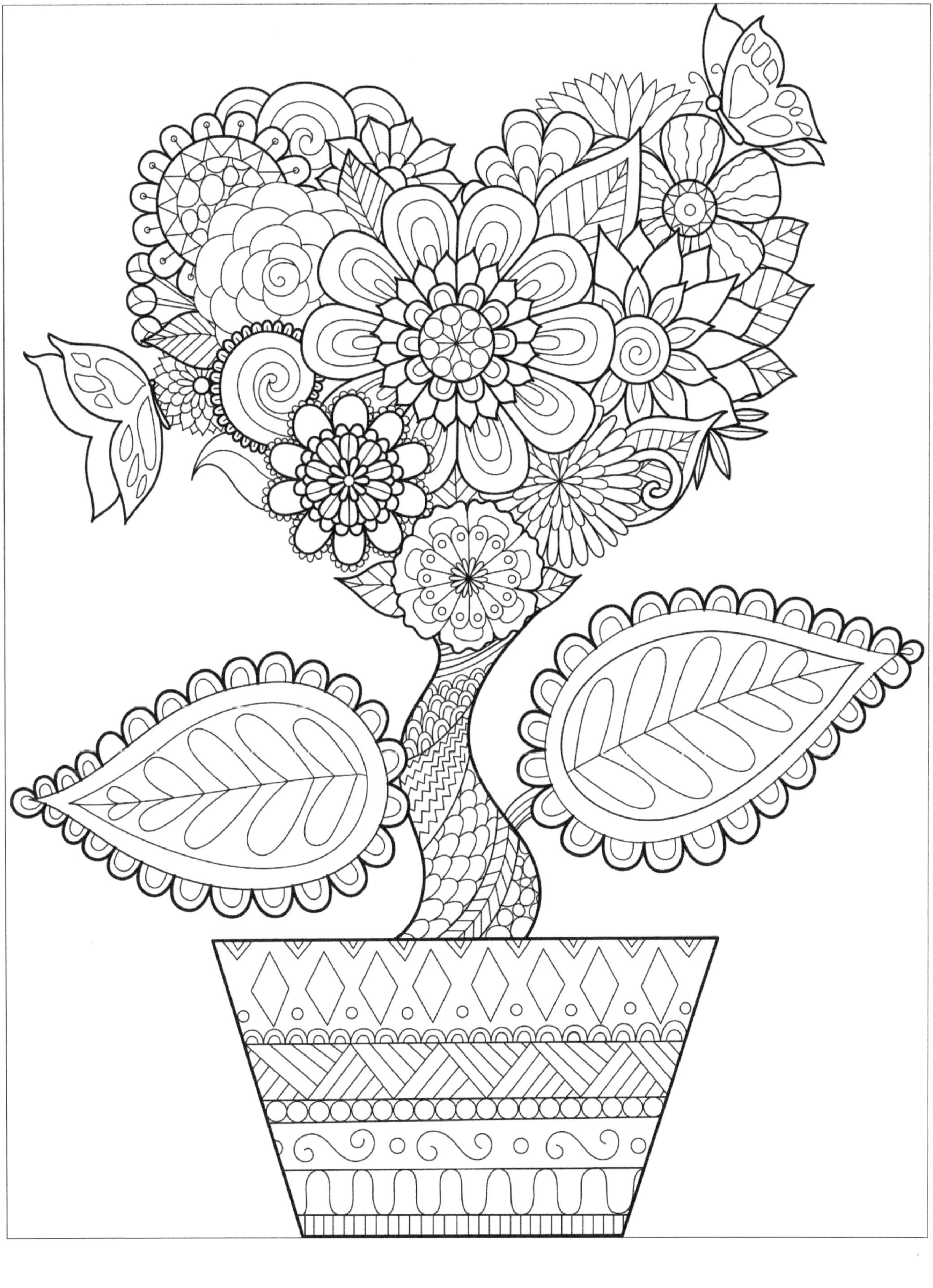

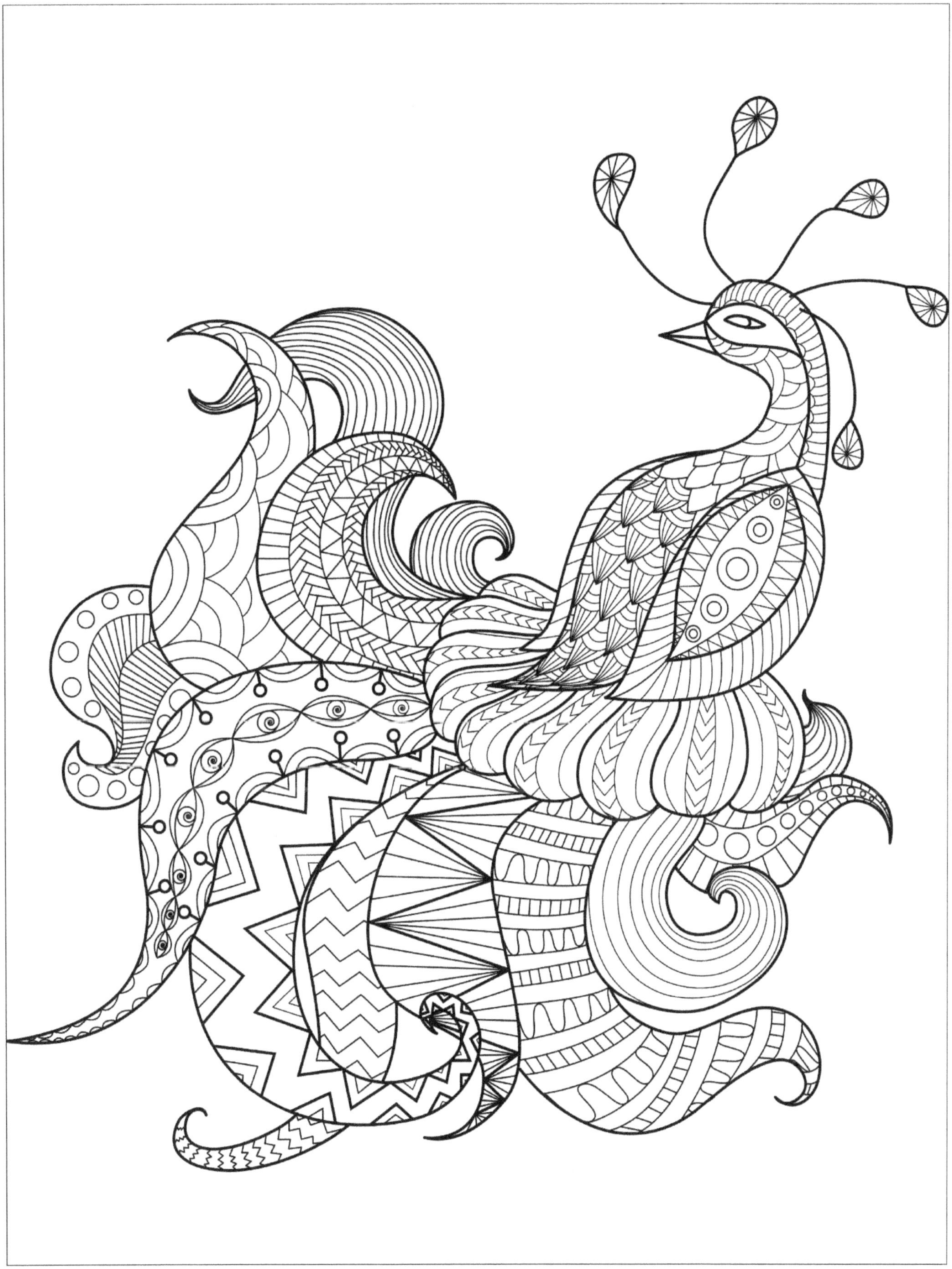

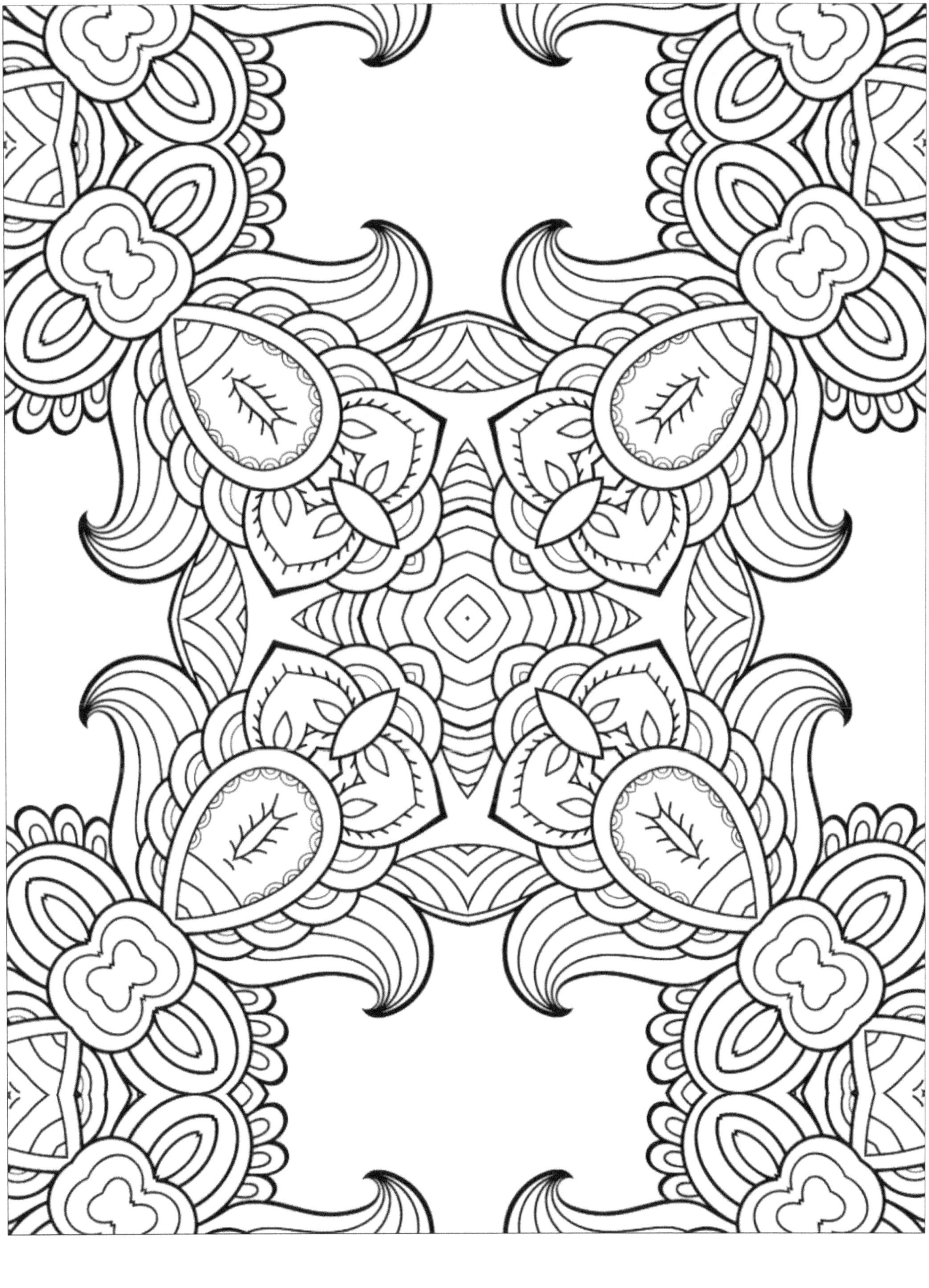

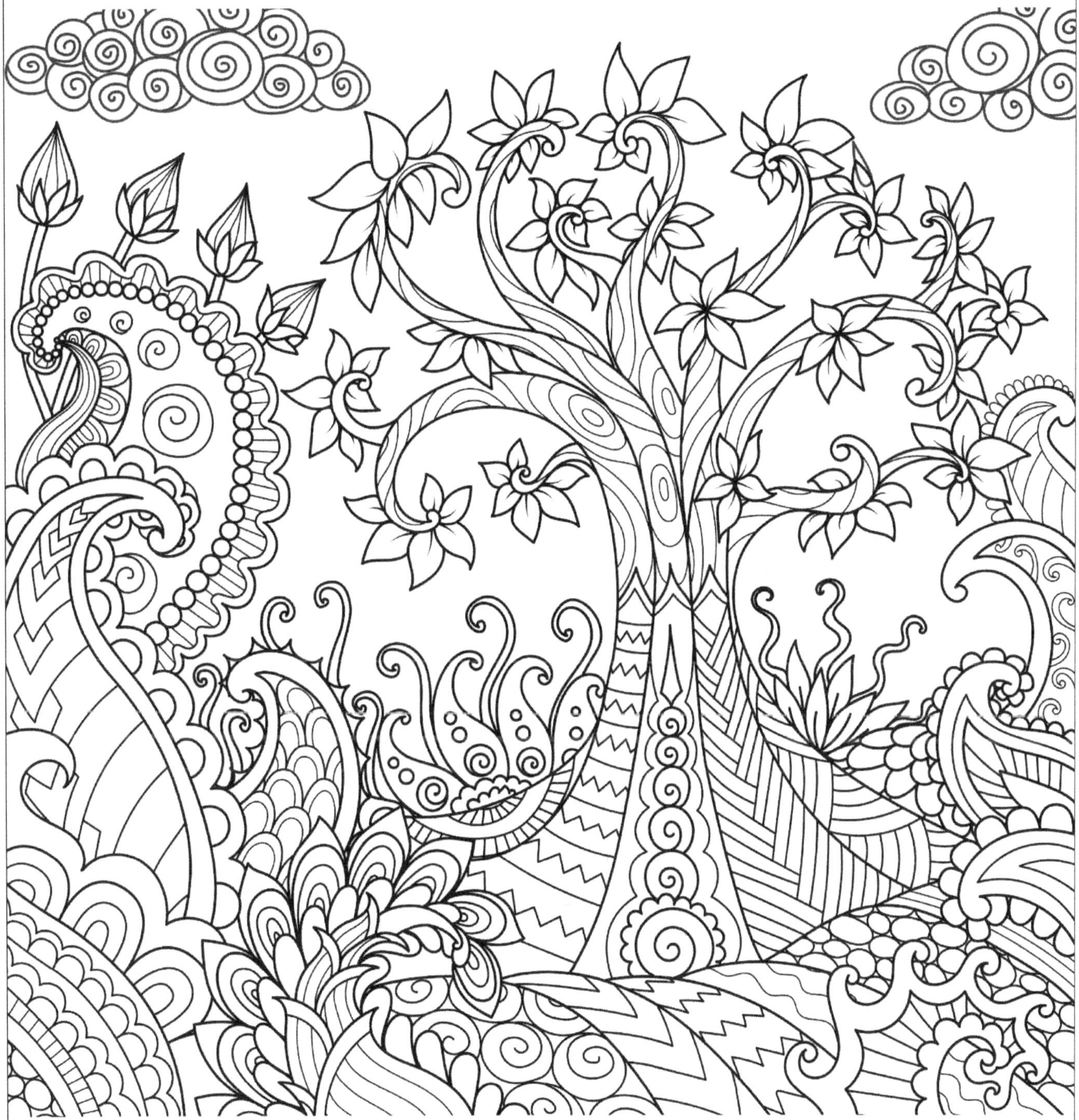

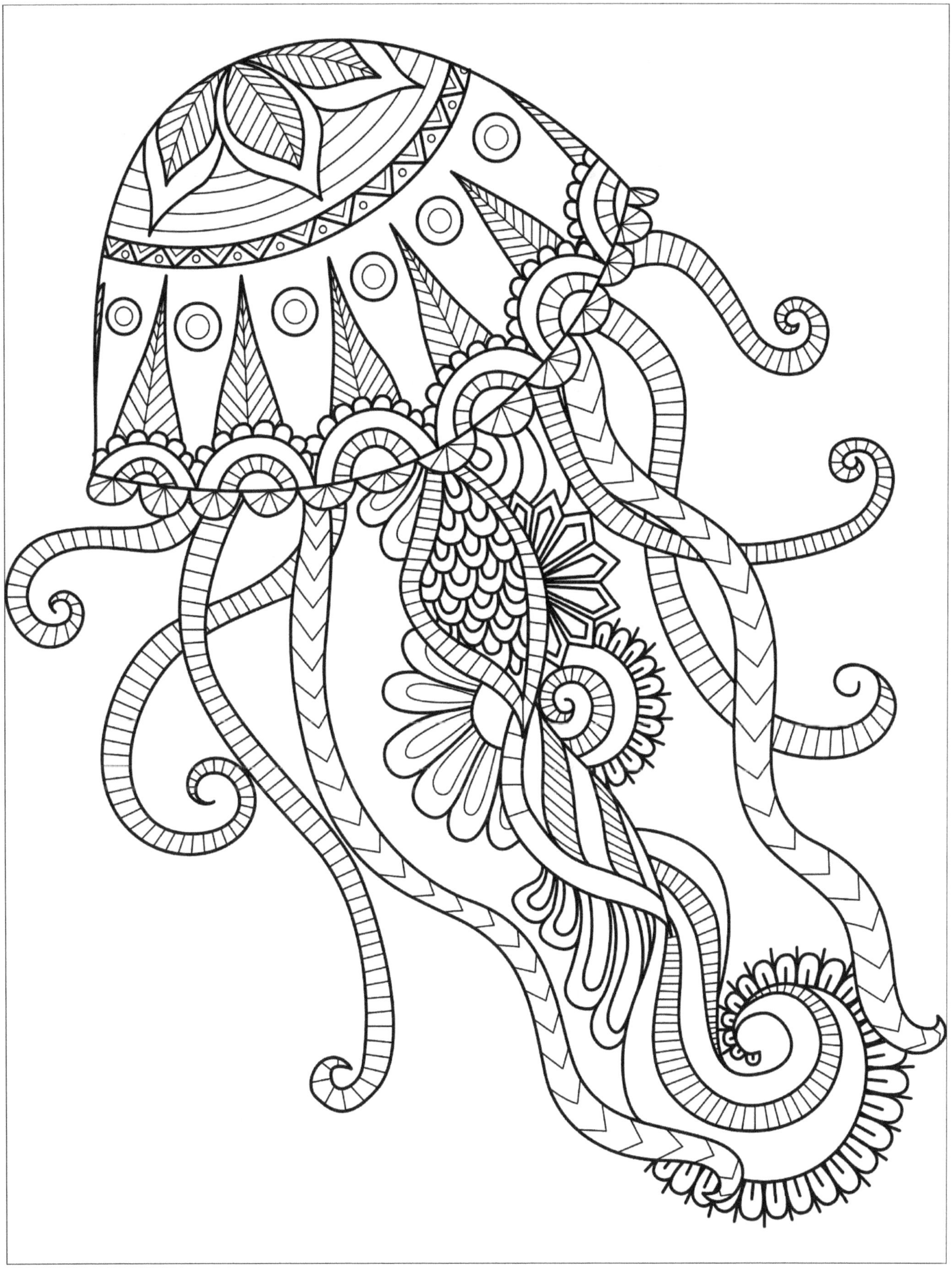

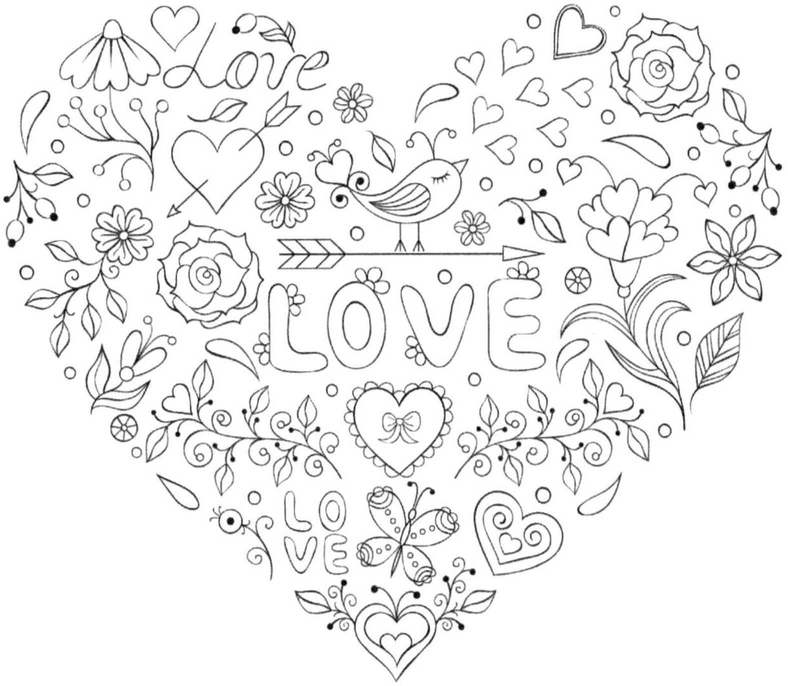
Love
LOVE
LO
VE

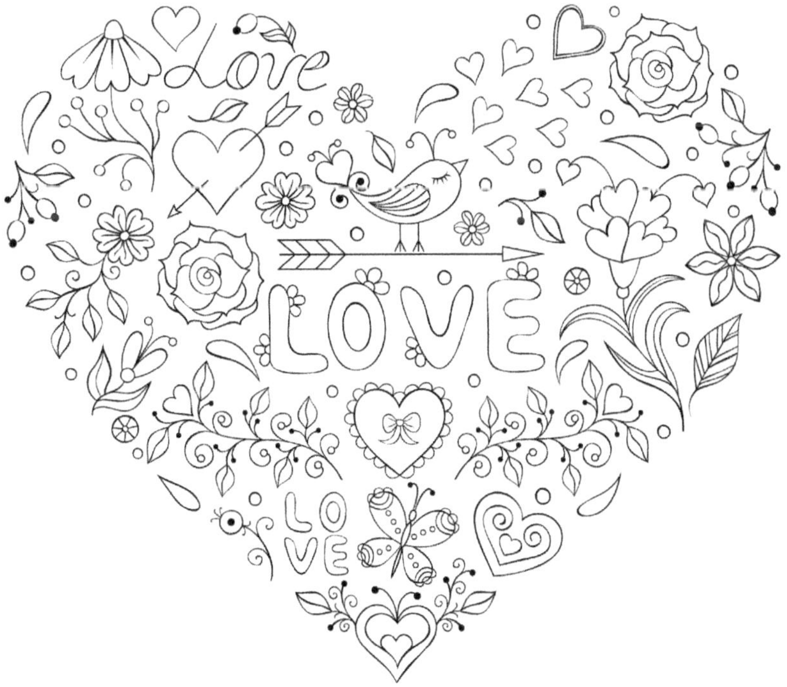
Love
LOVE
LO
VE

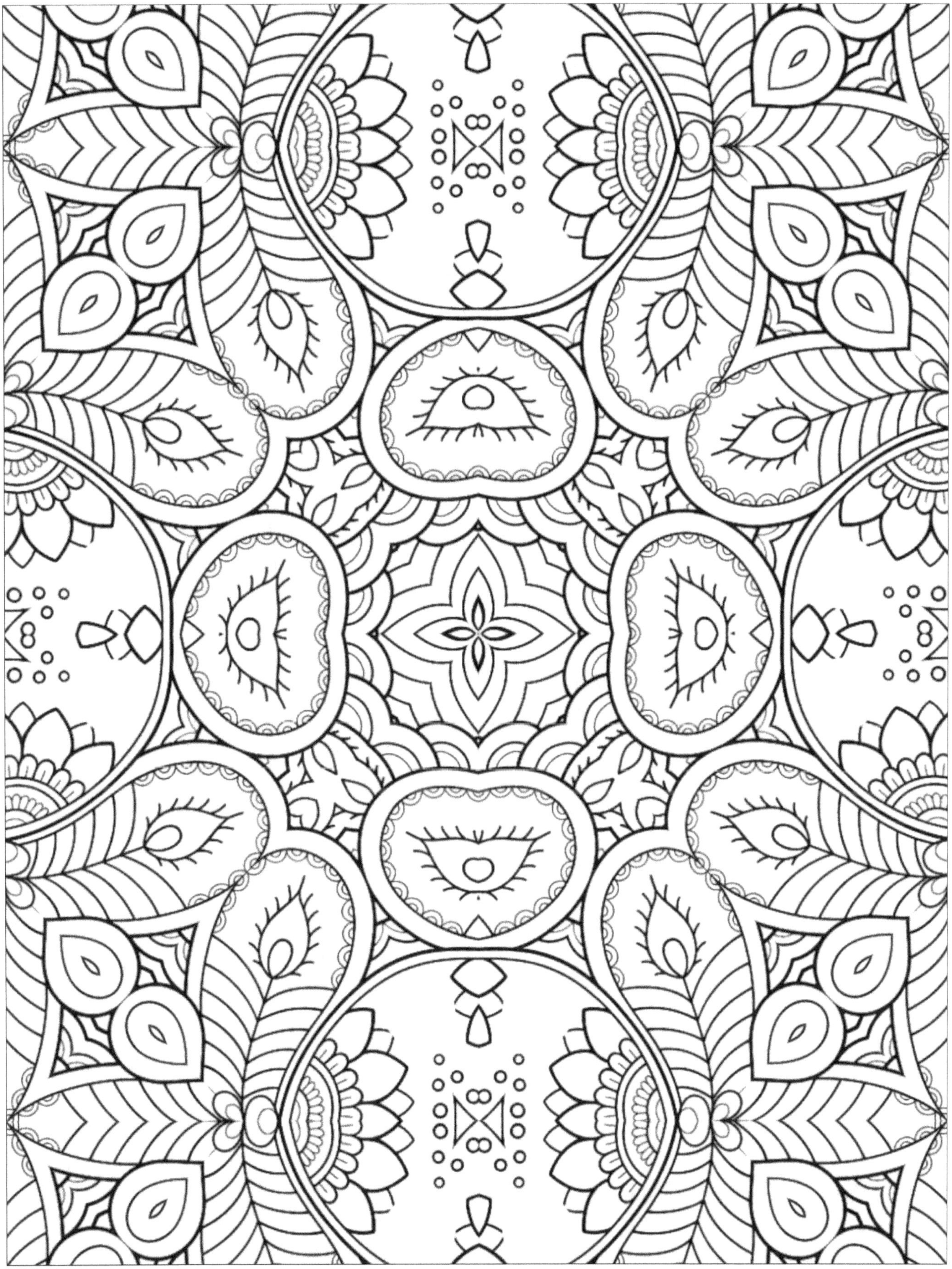

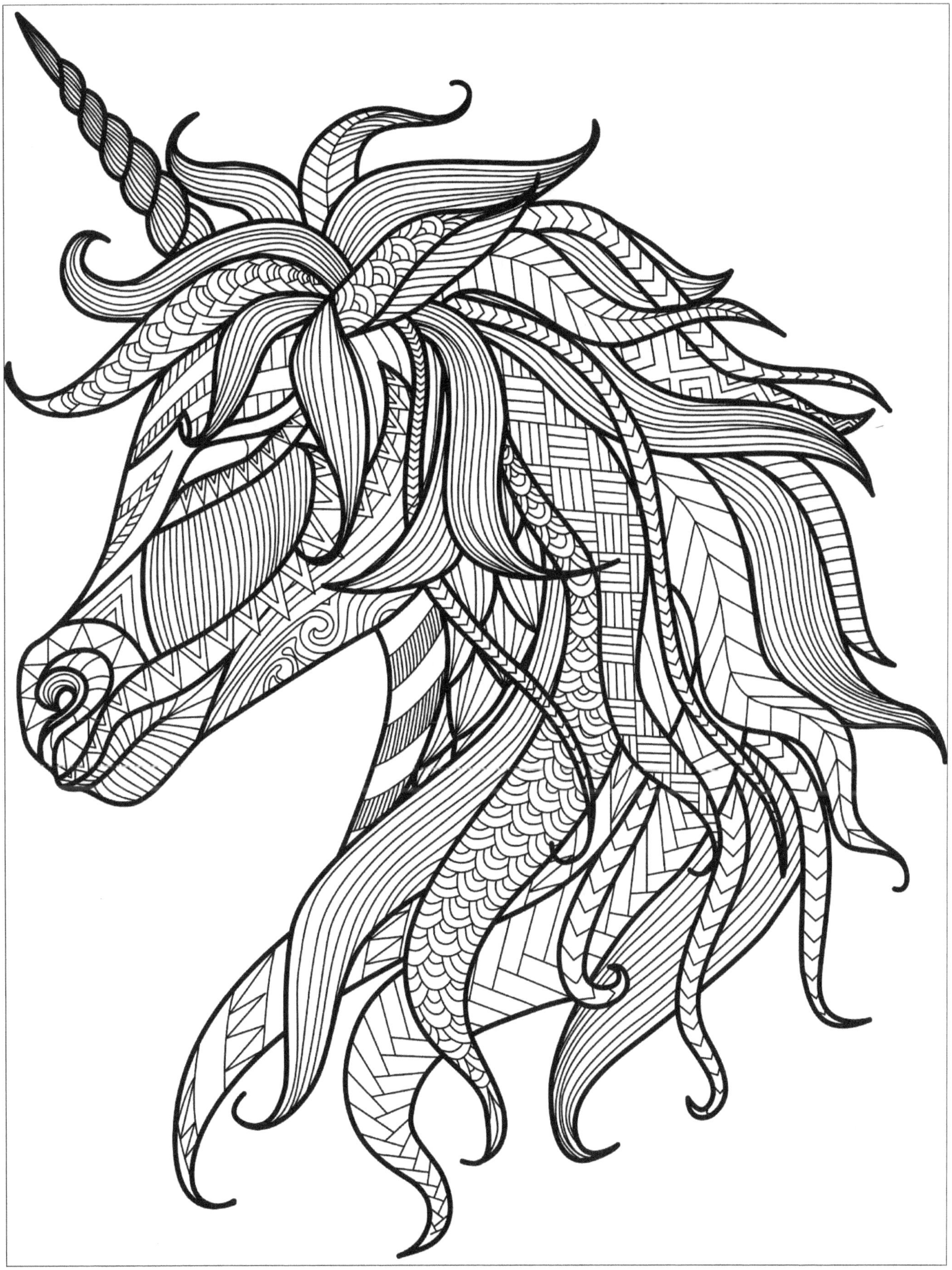

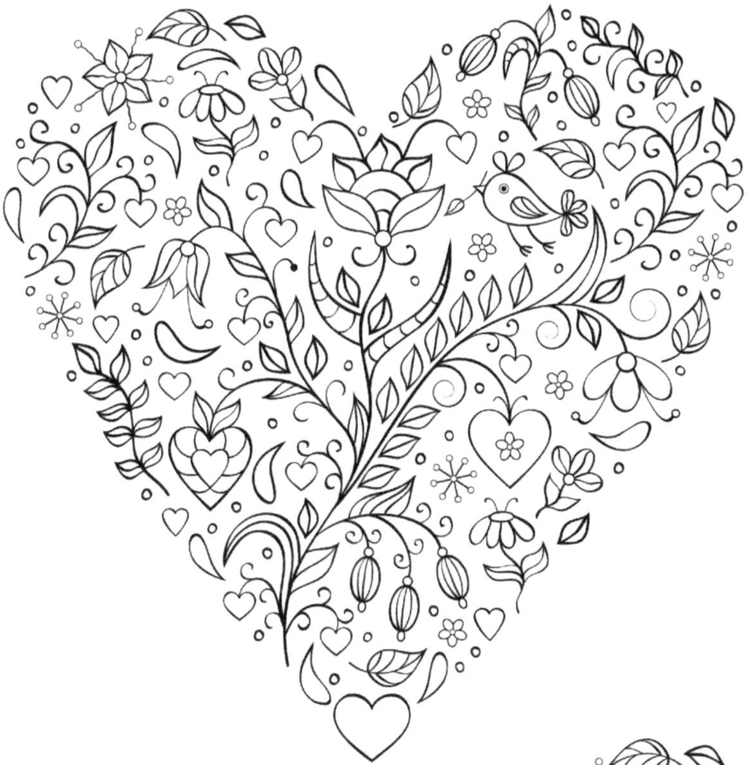
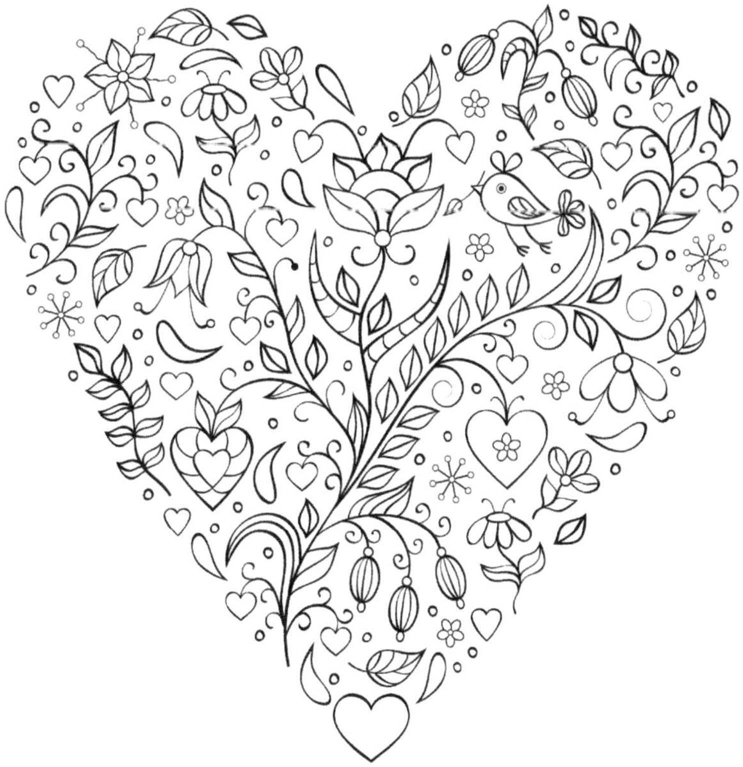

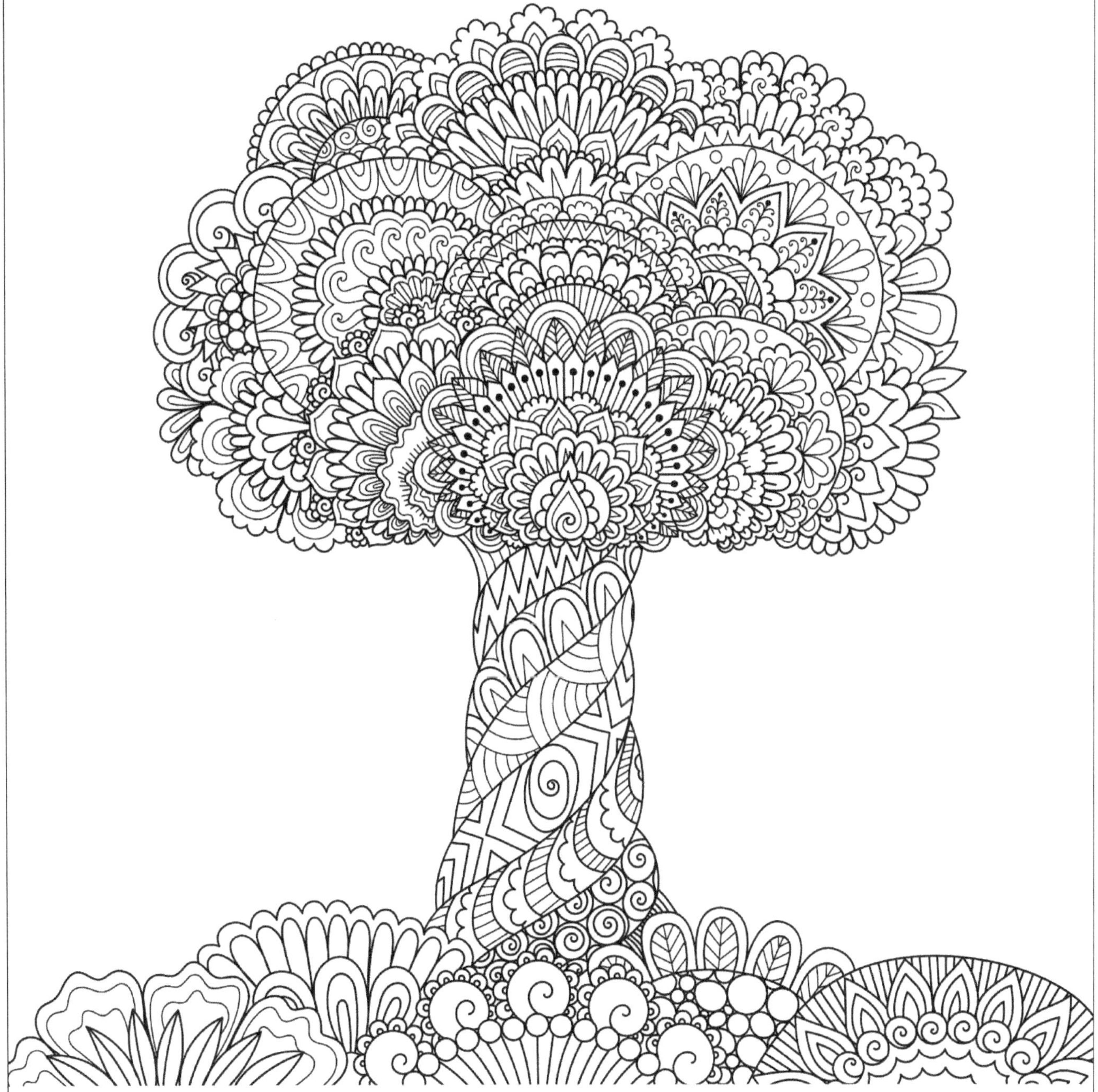

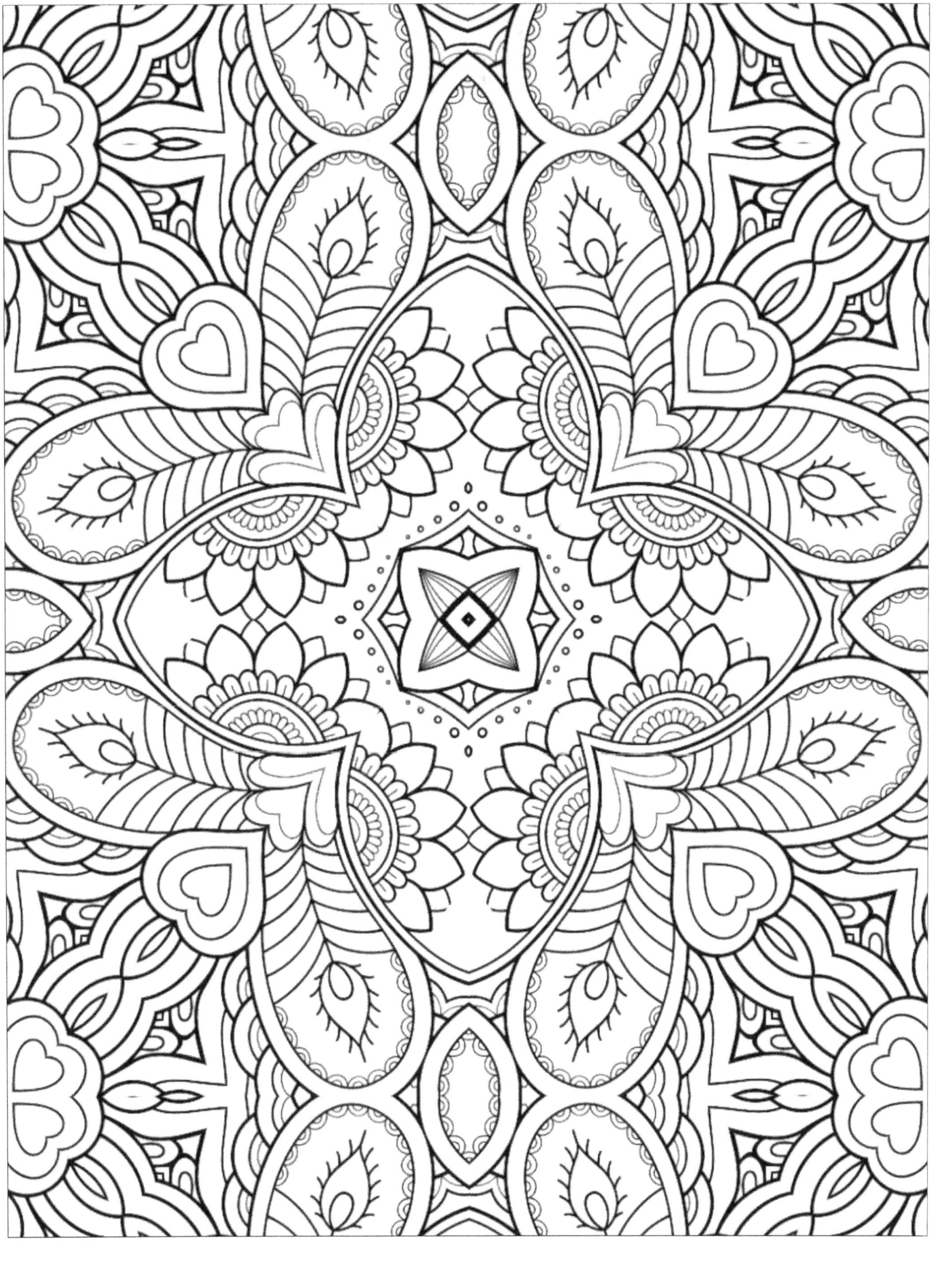

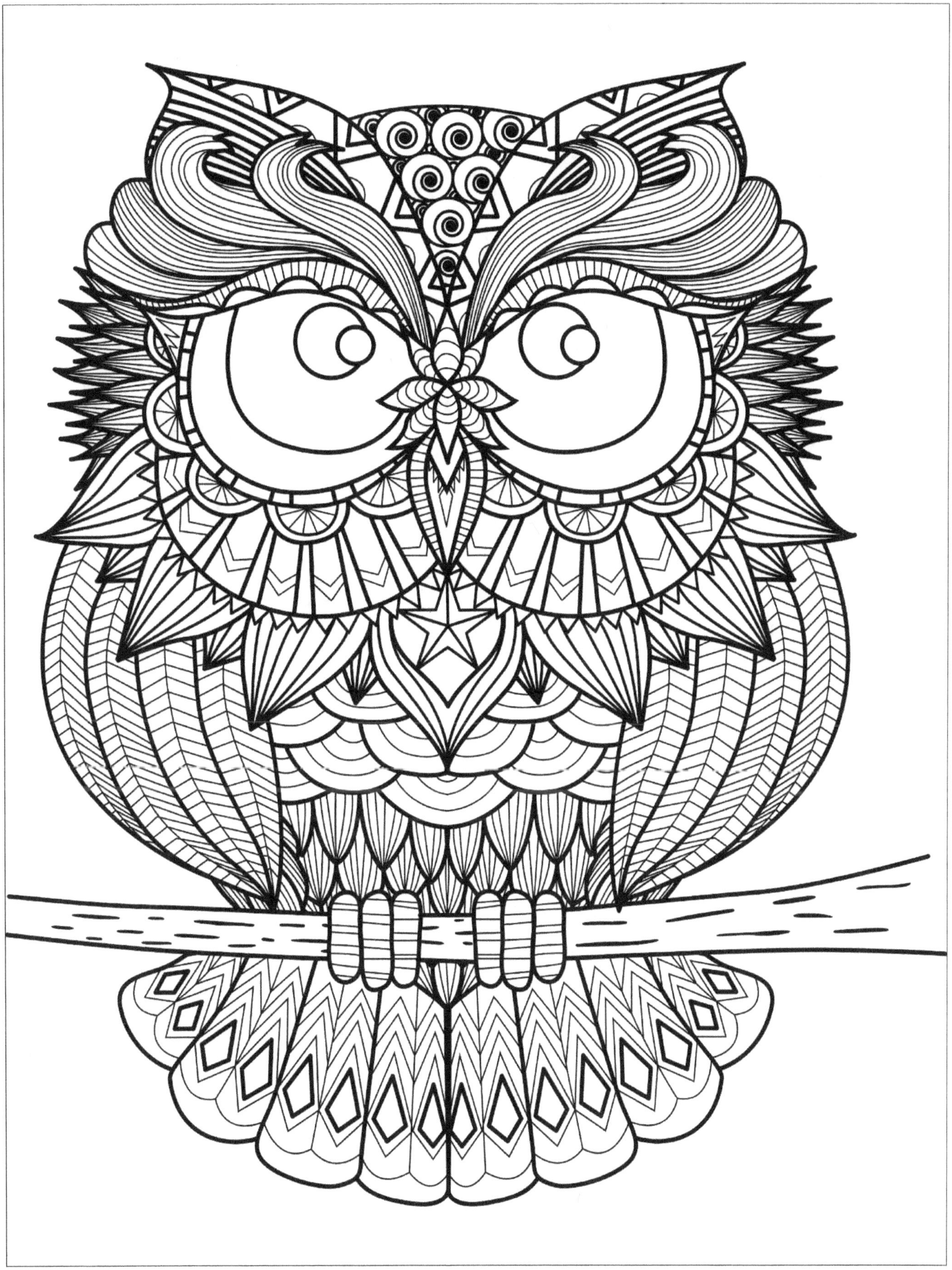

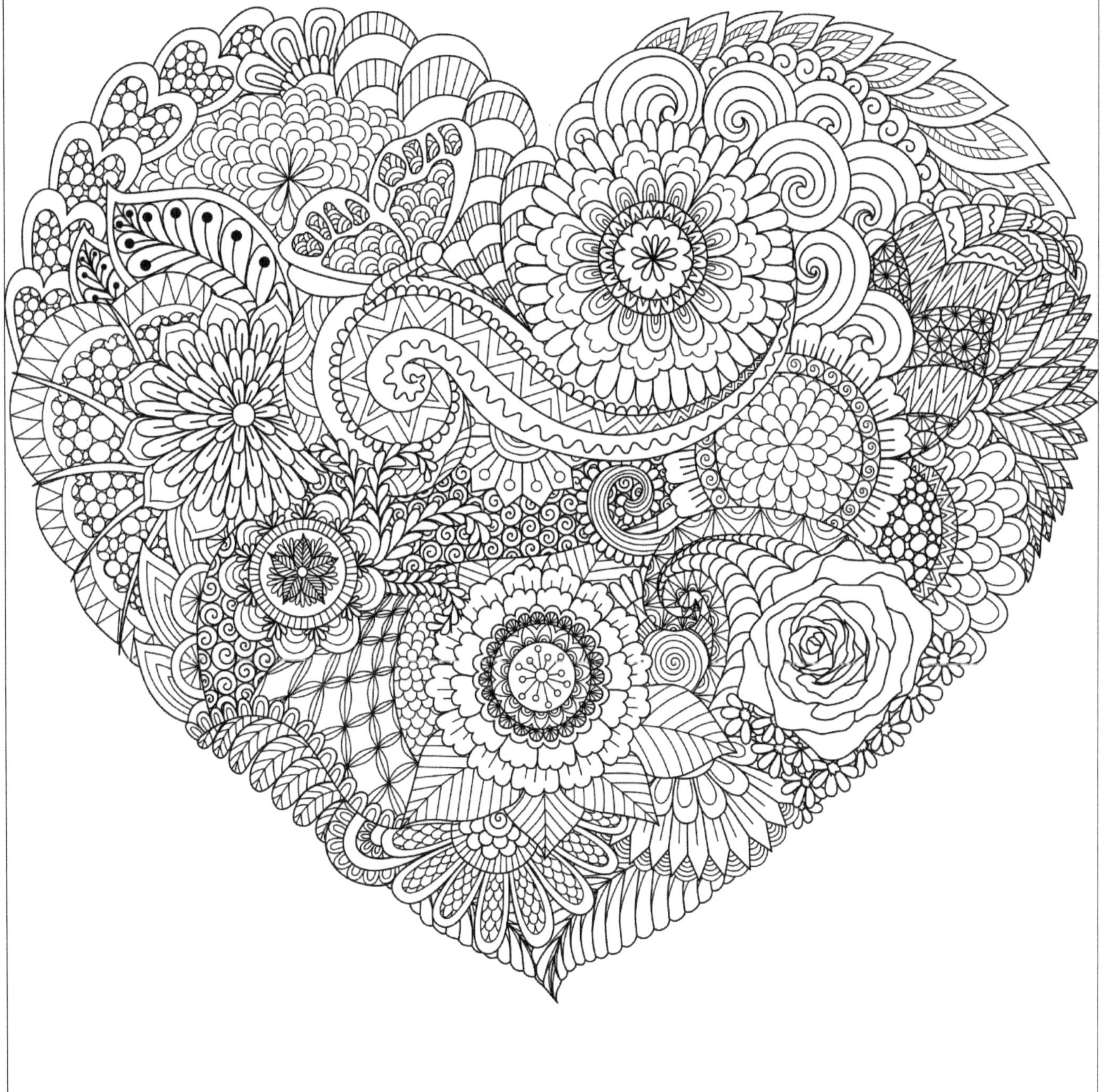

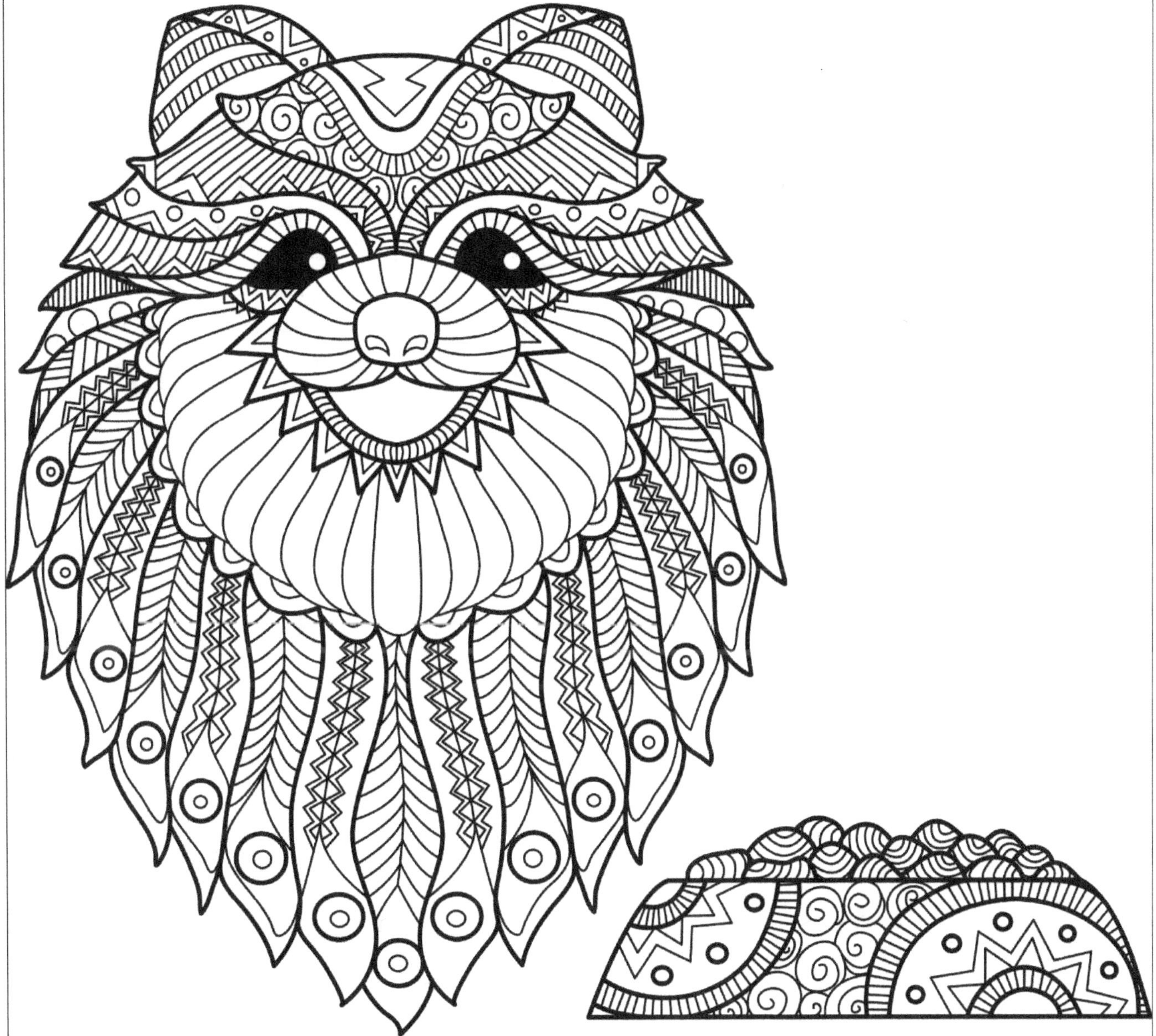

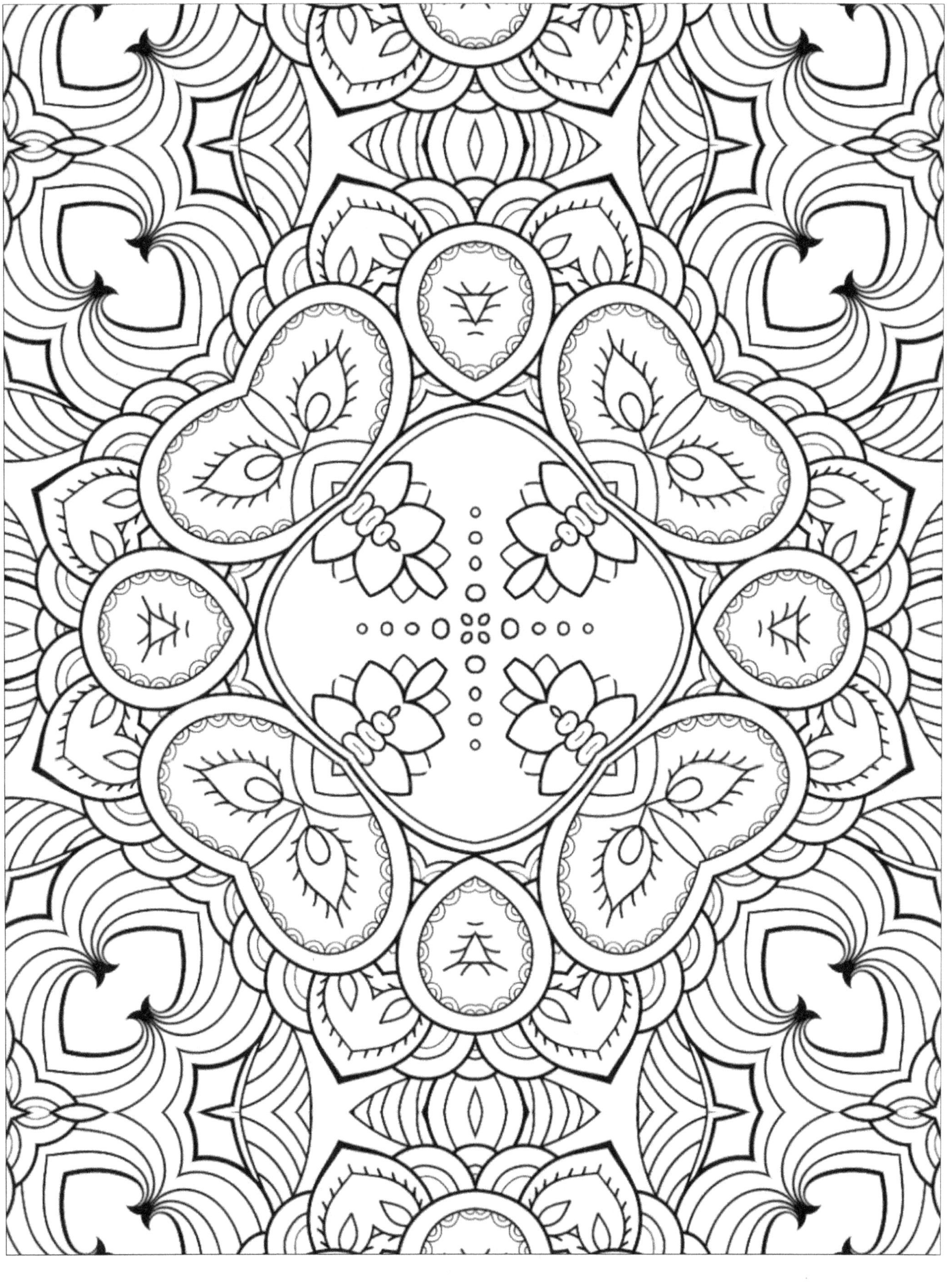

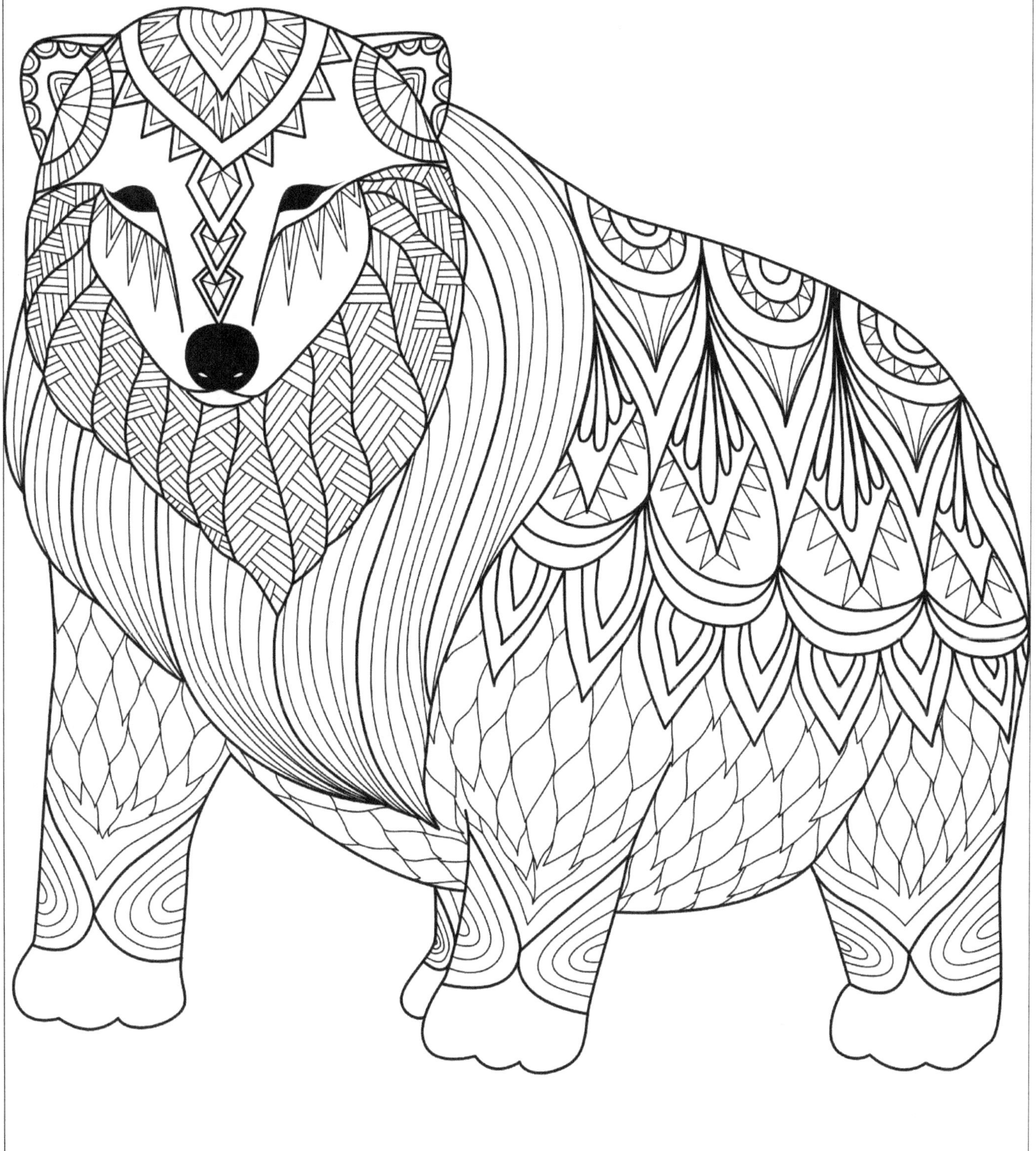

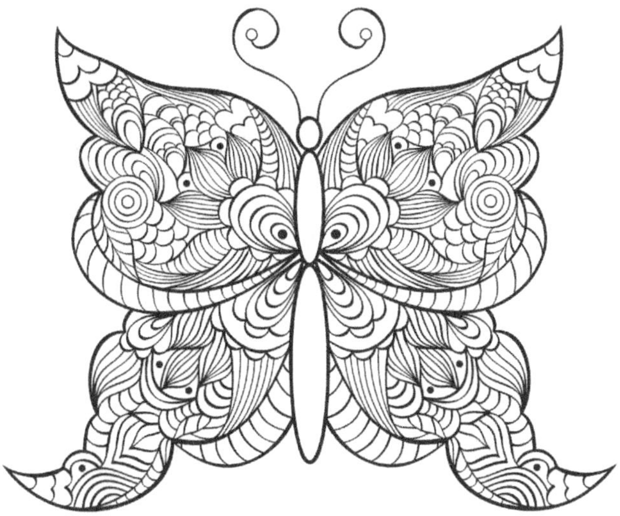

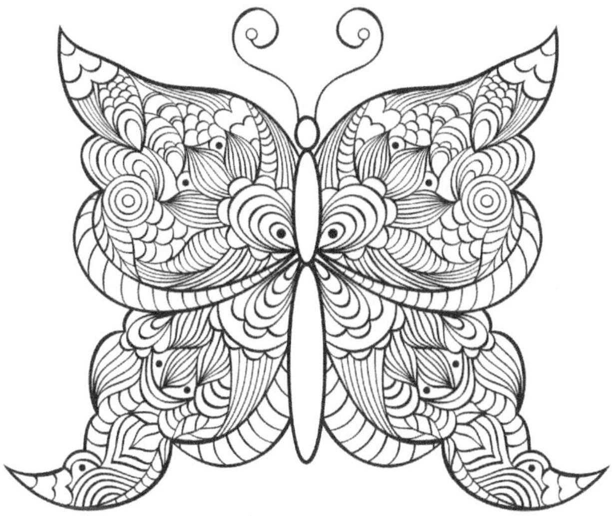

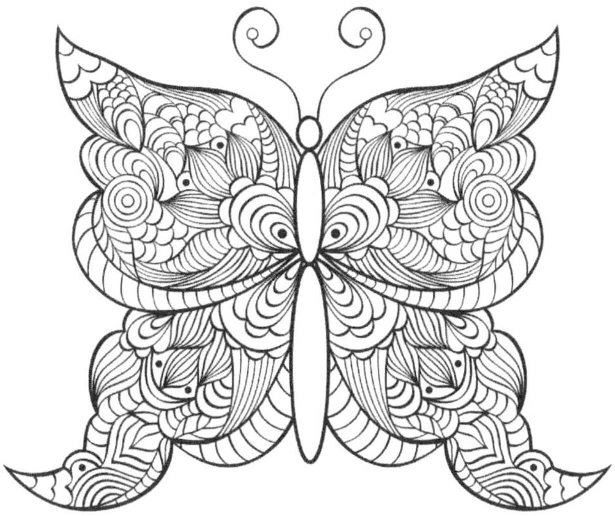

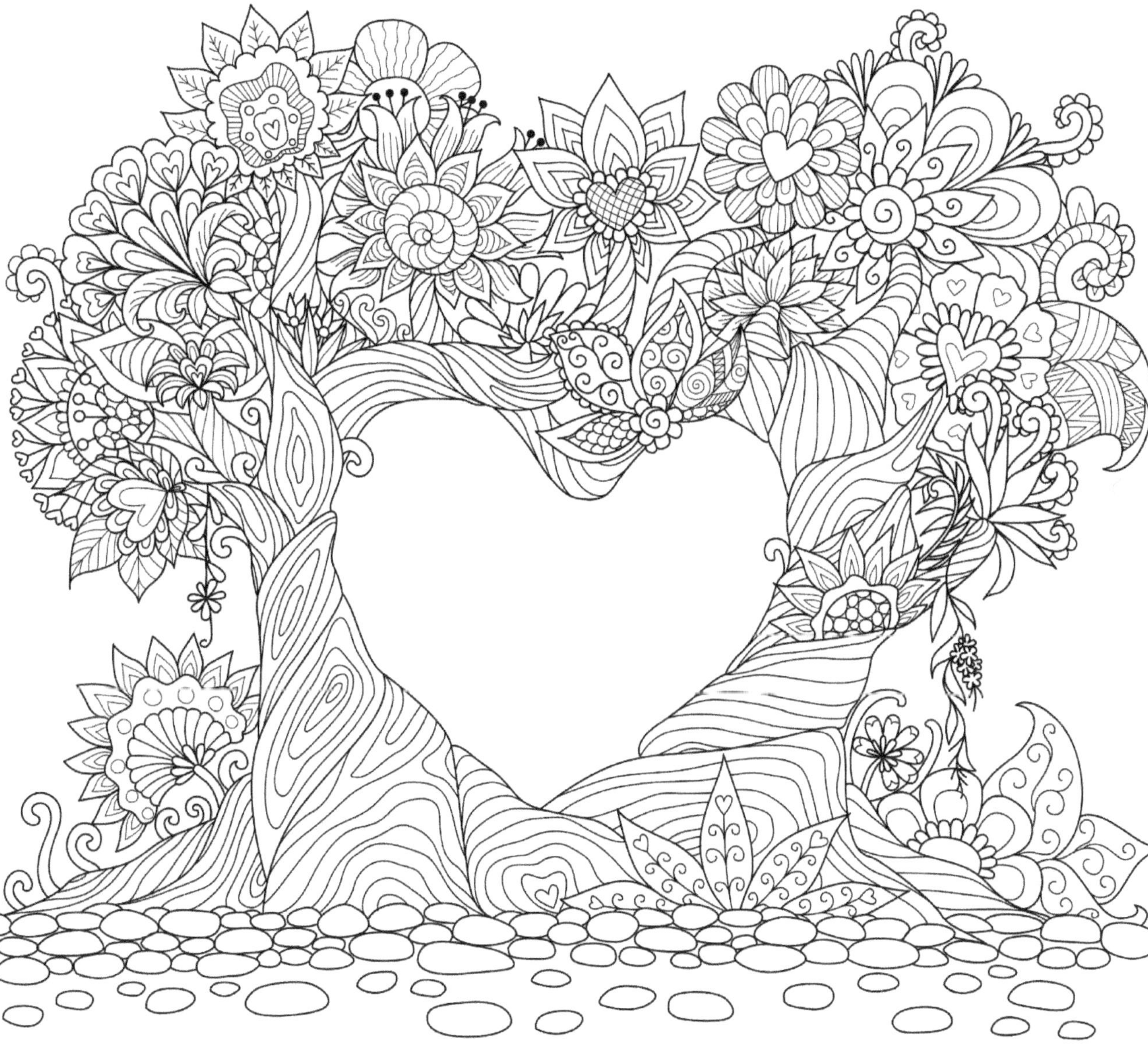

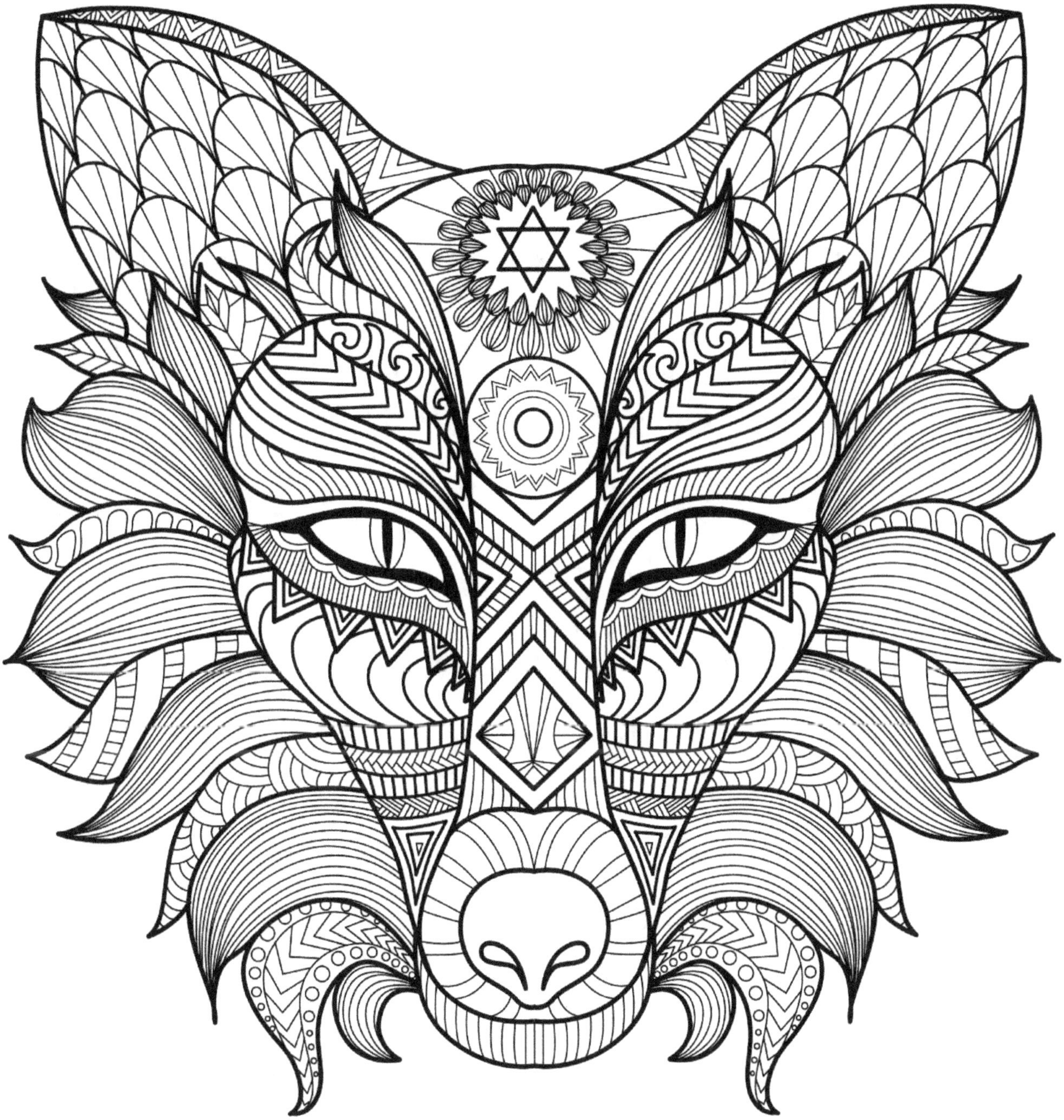

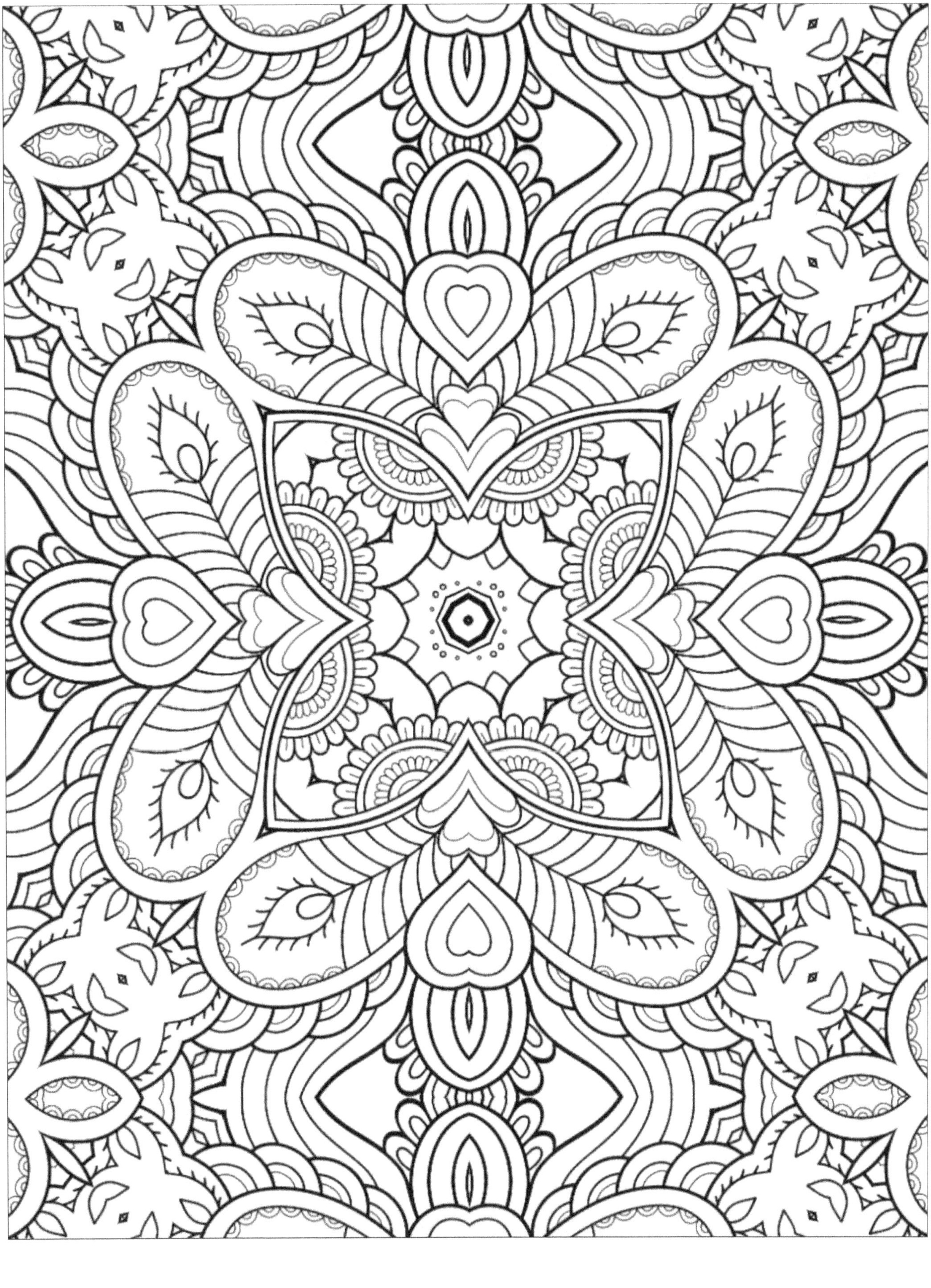

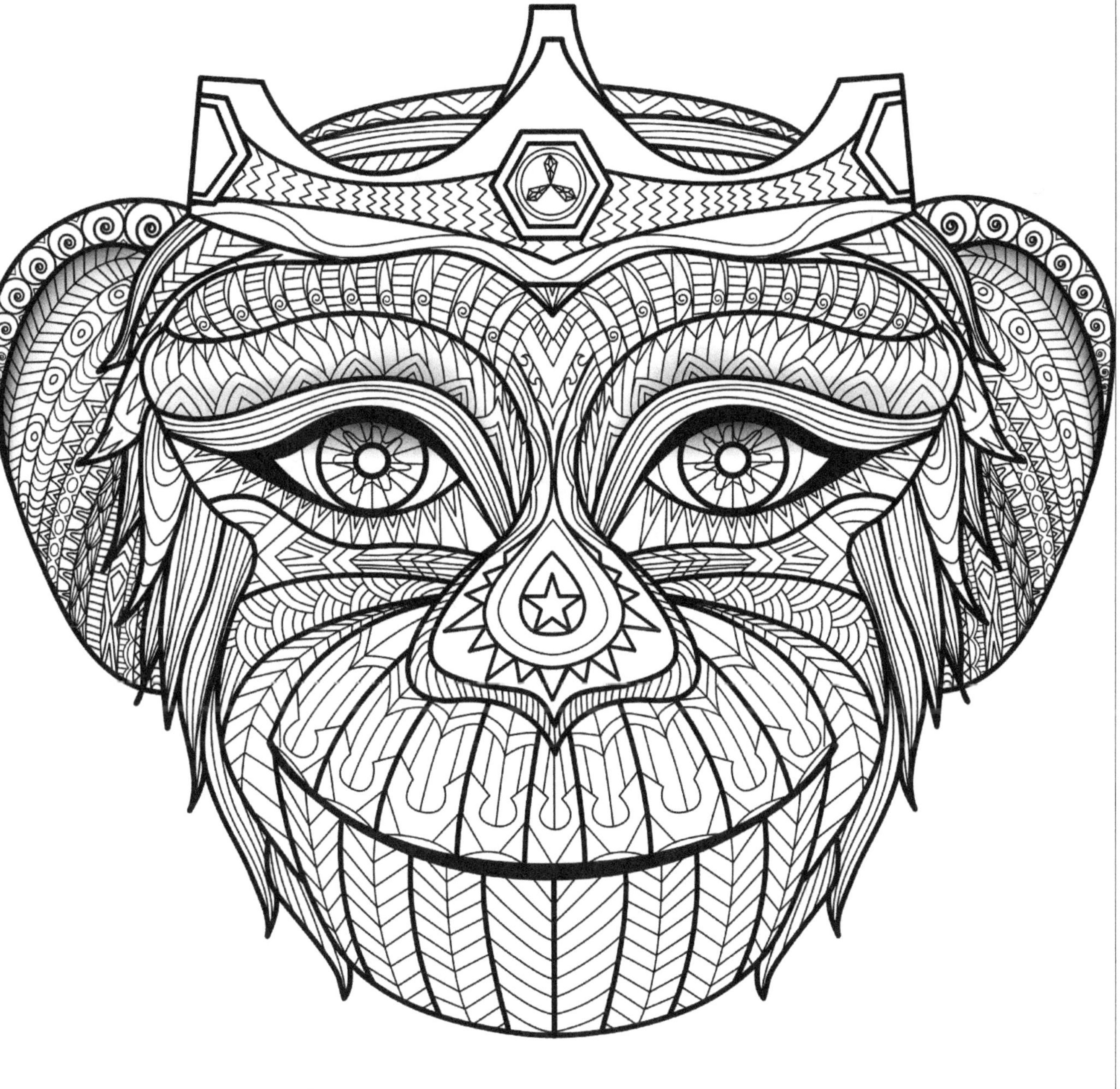

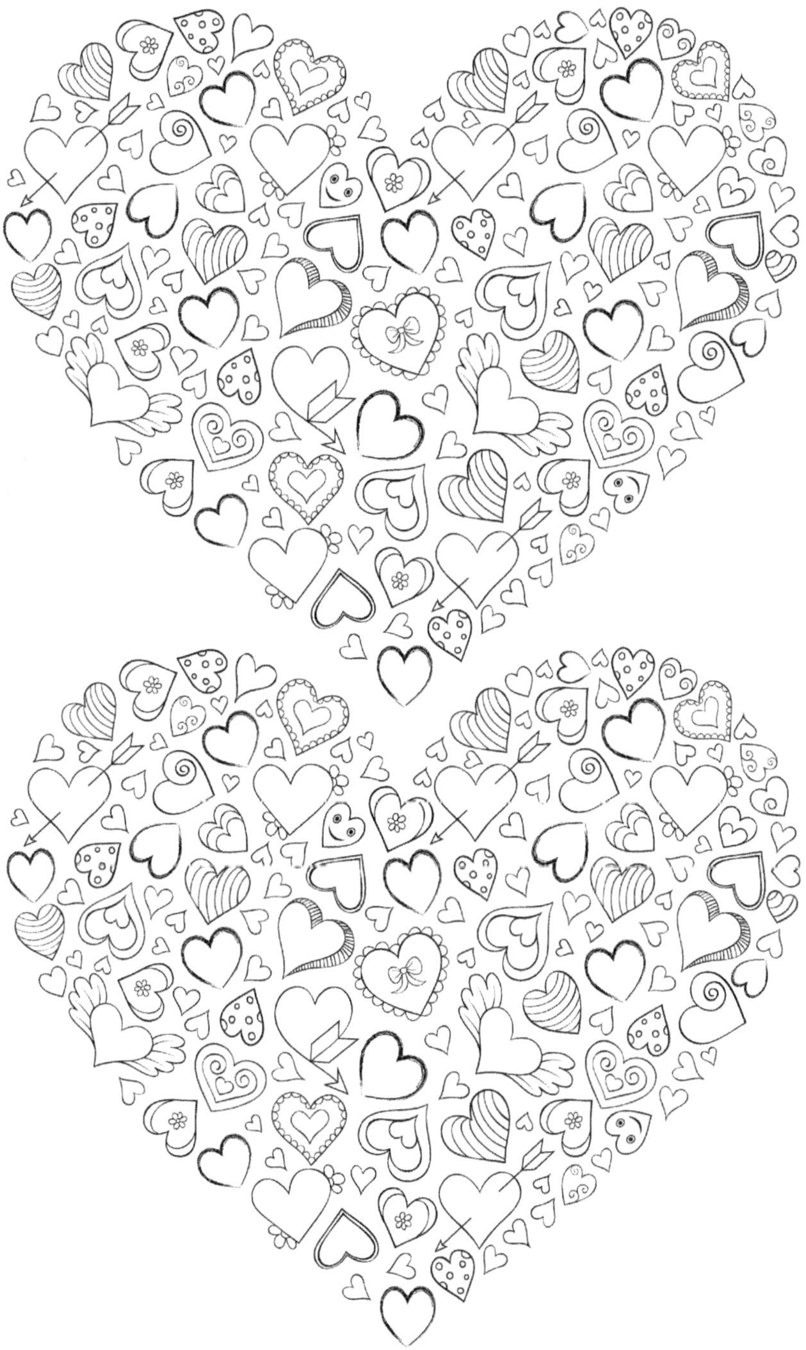

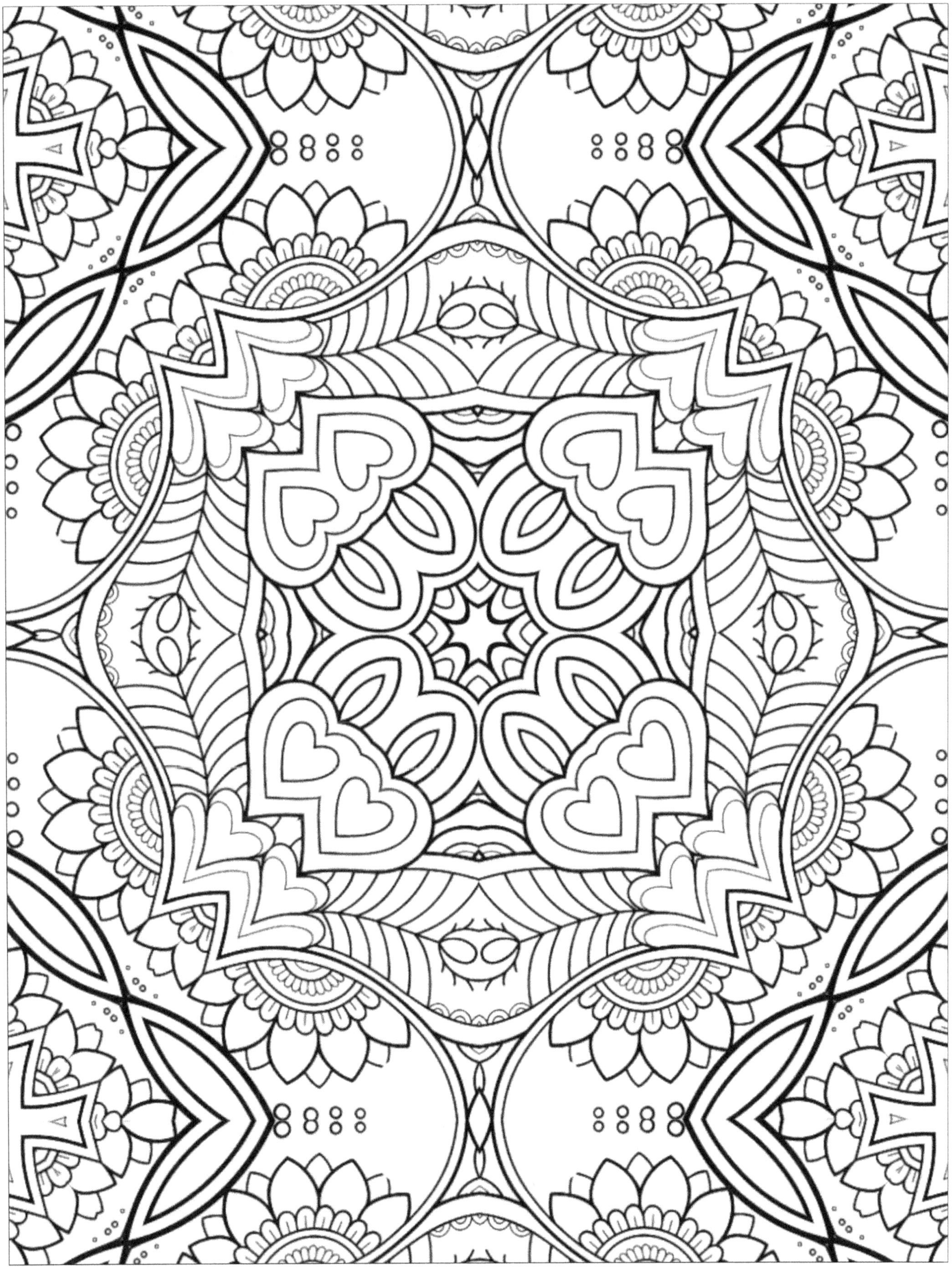

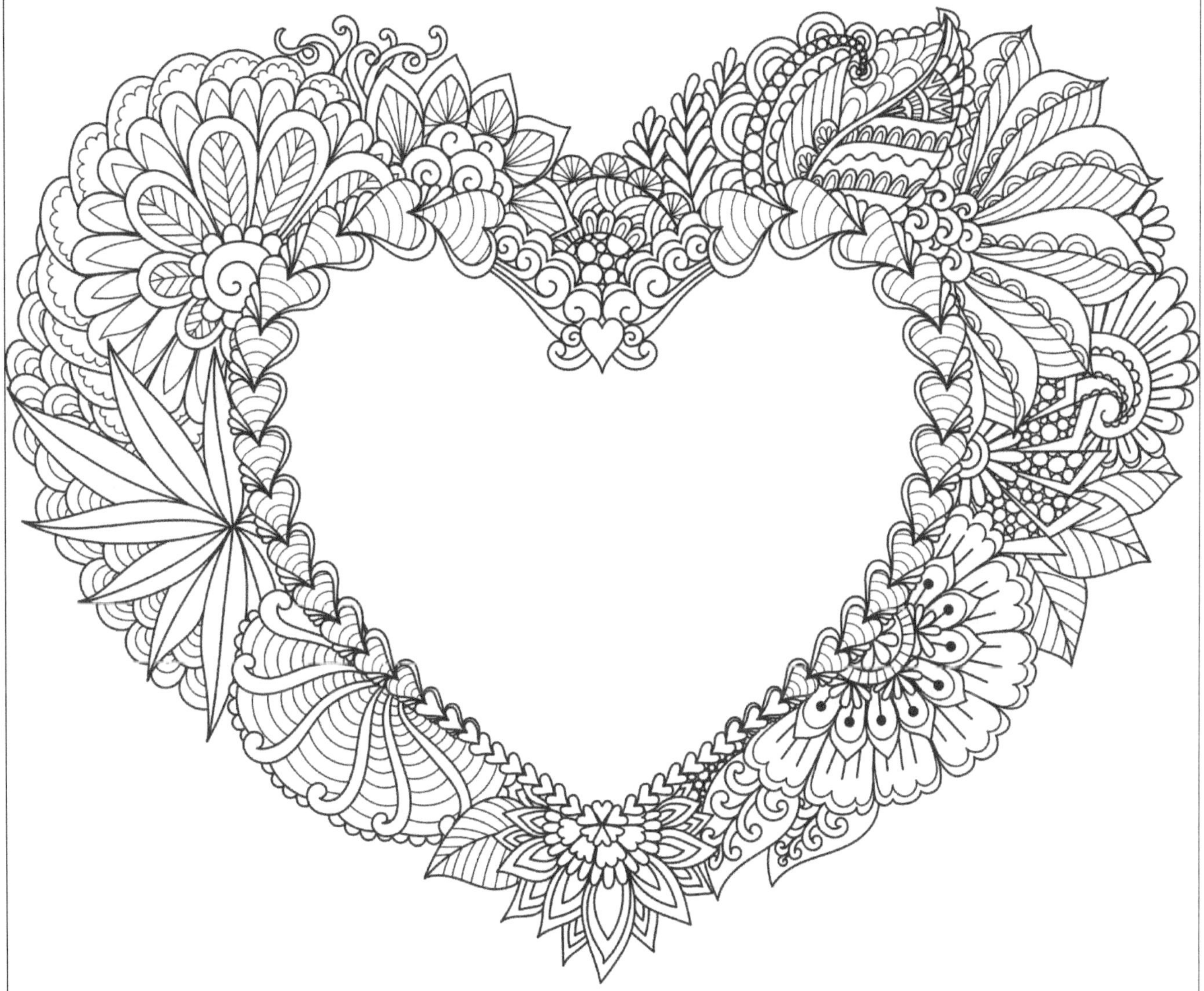

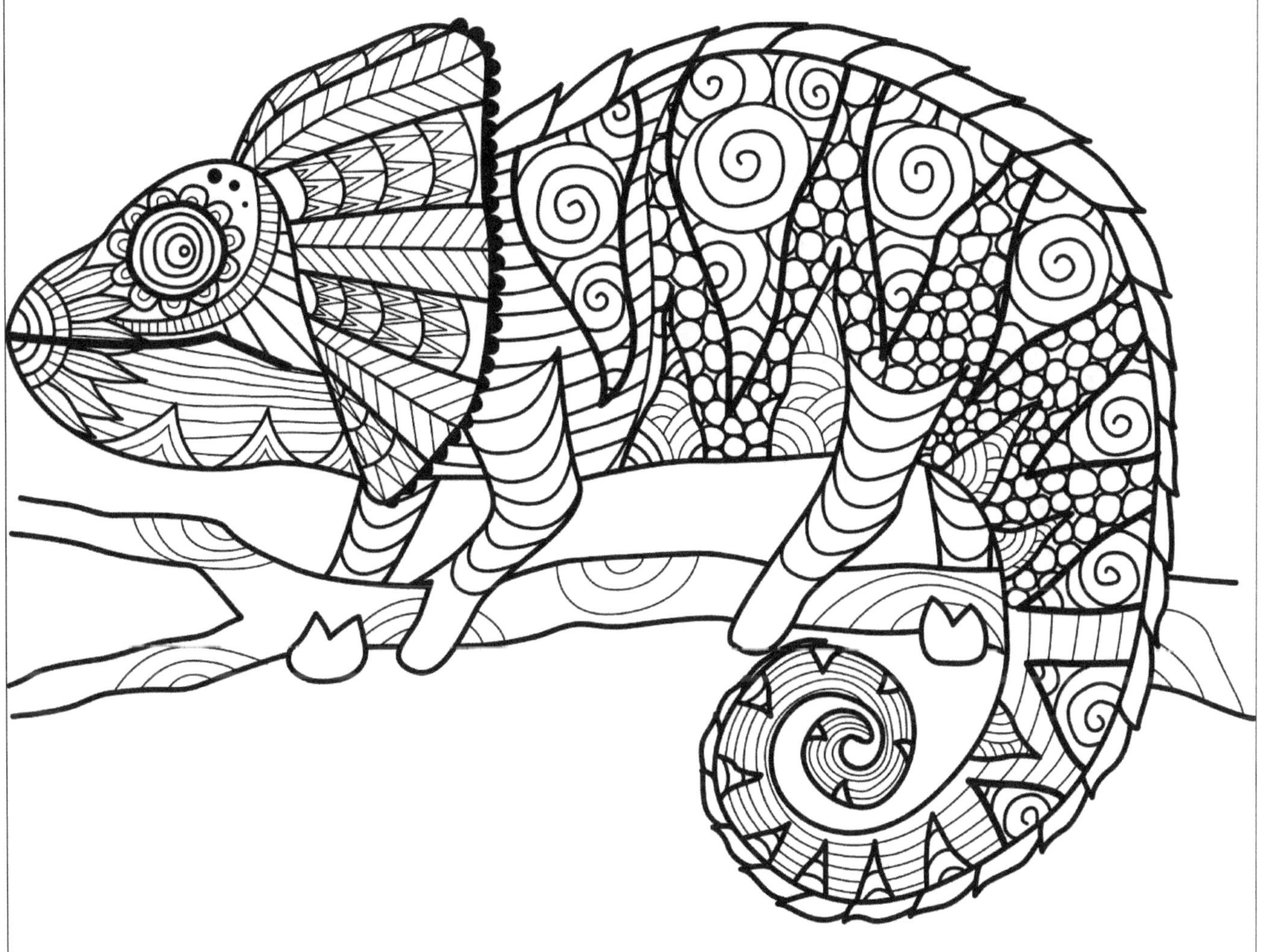

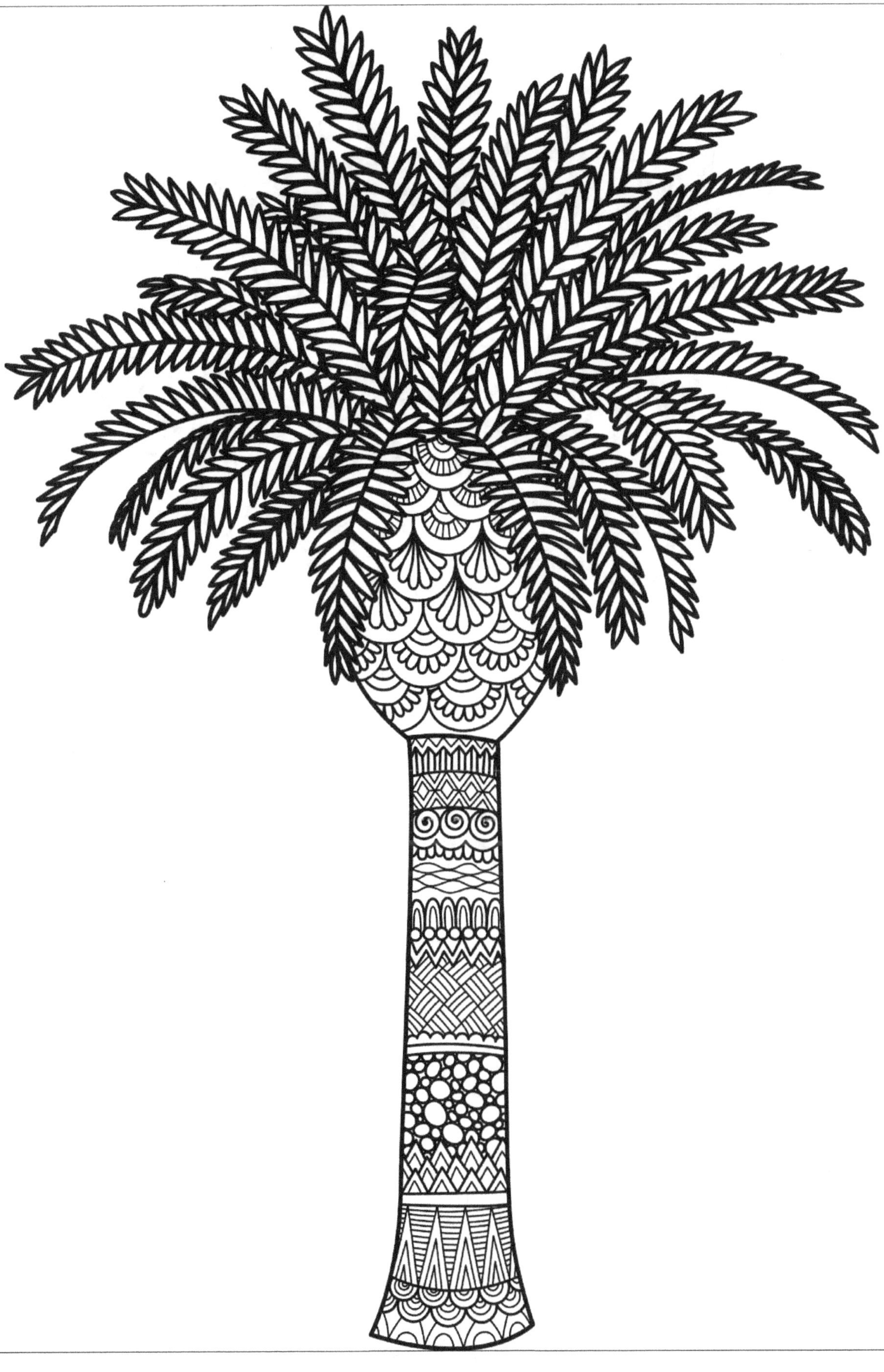

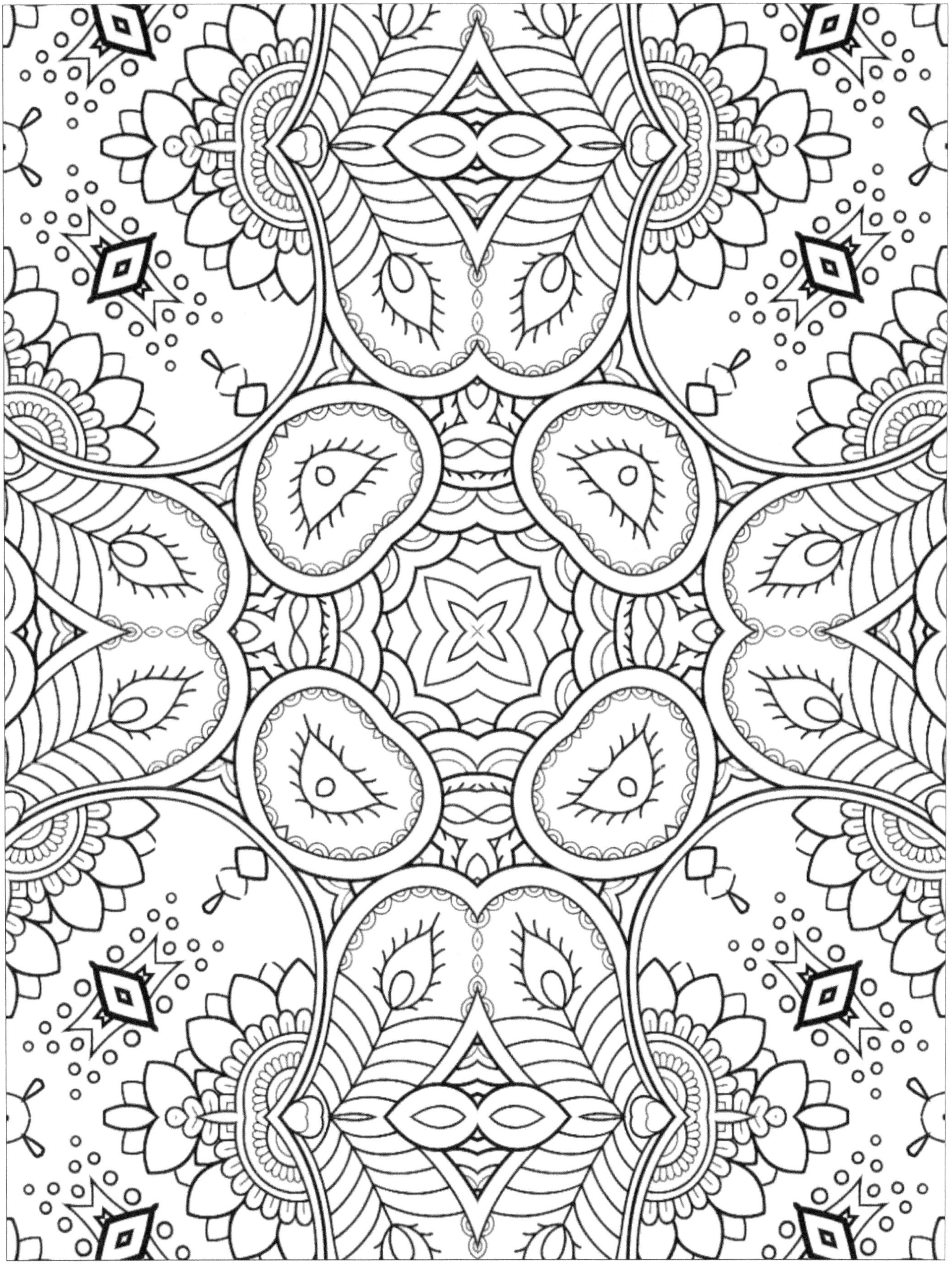

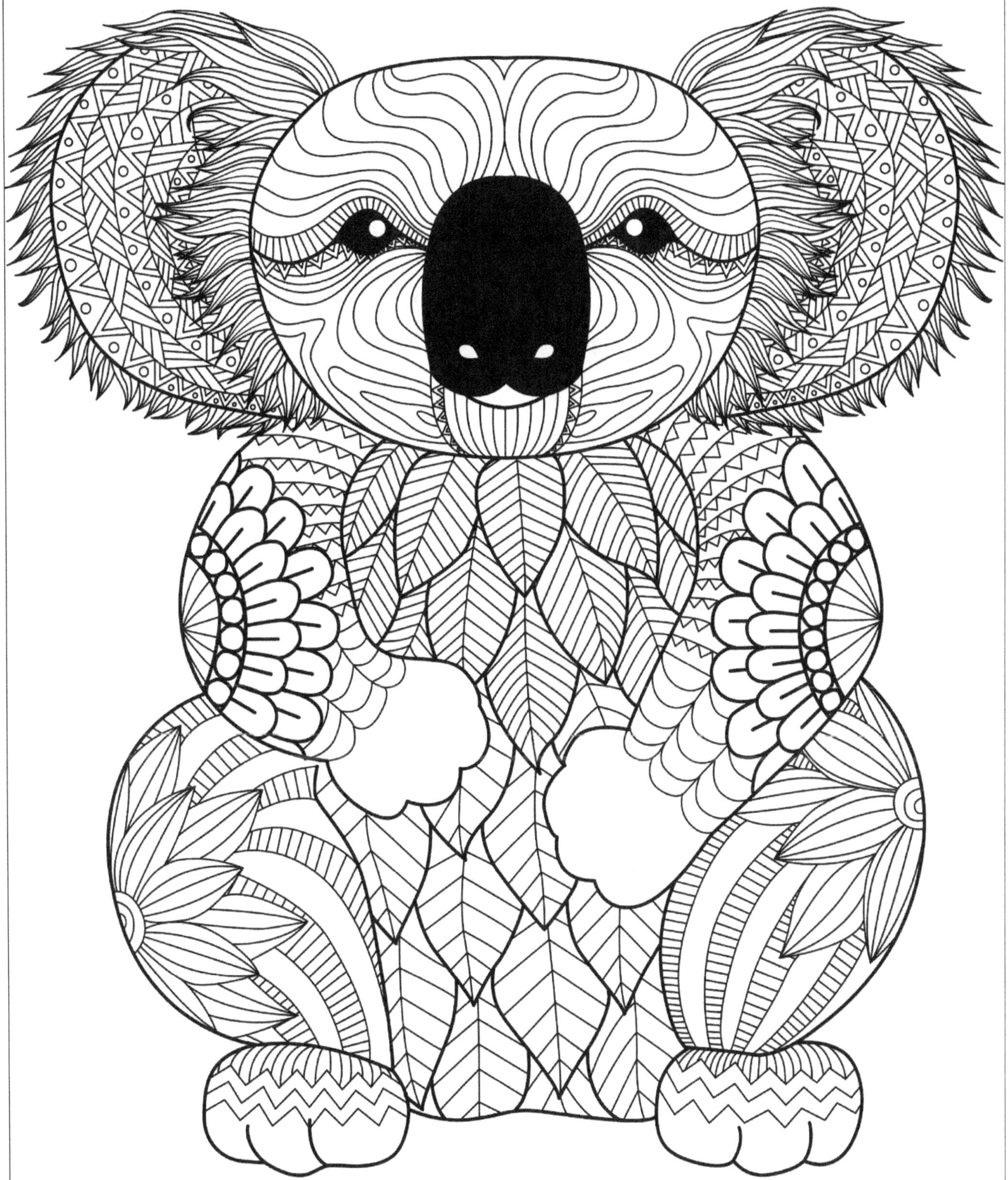

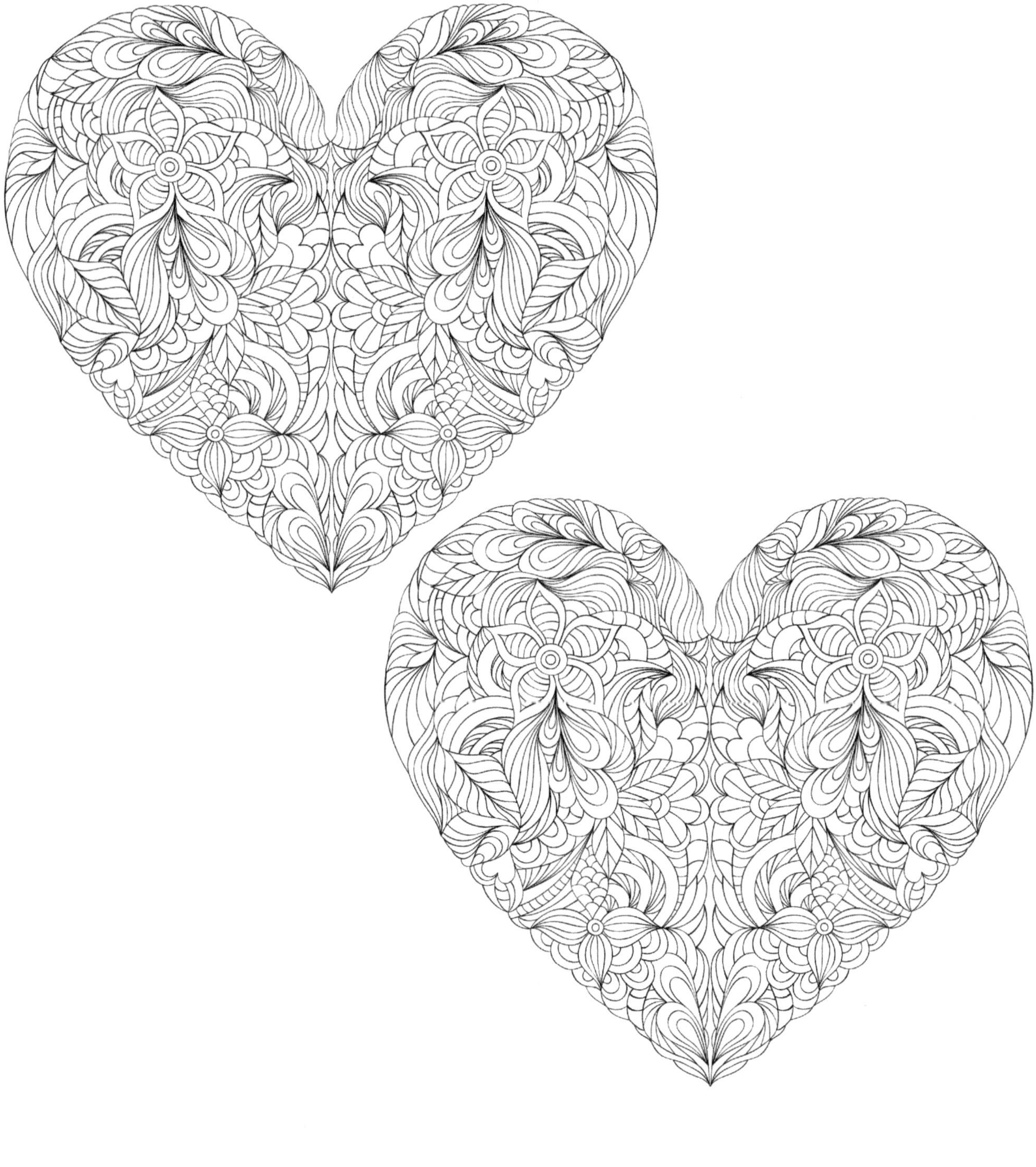

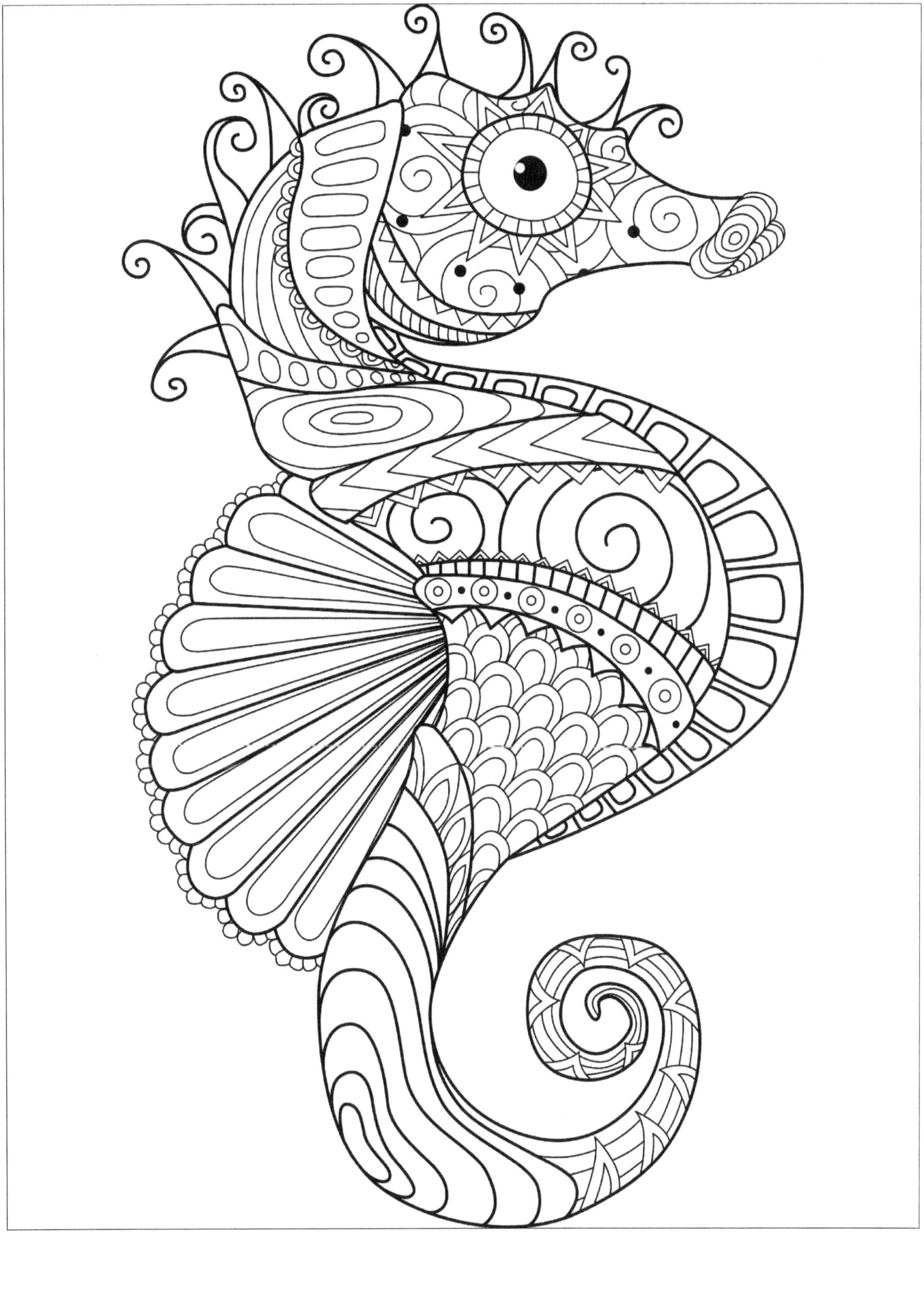

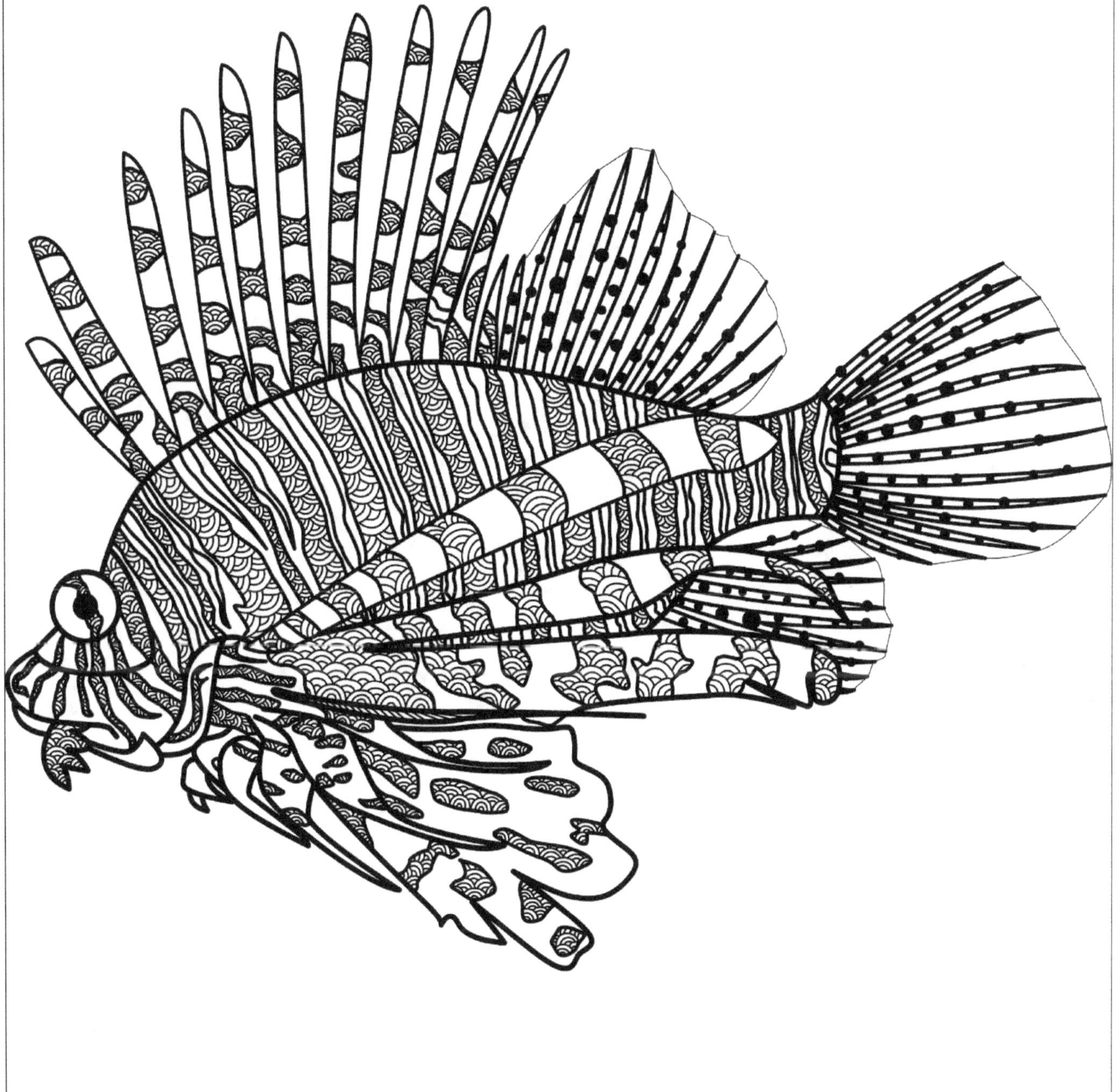

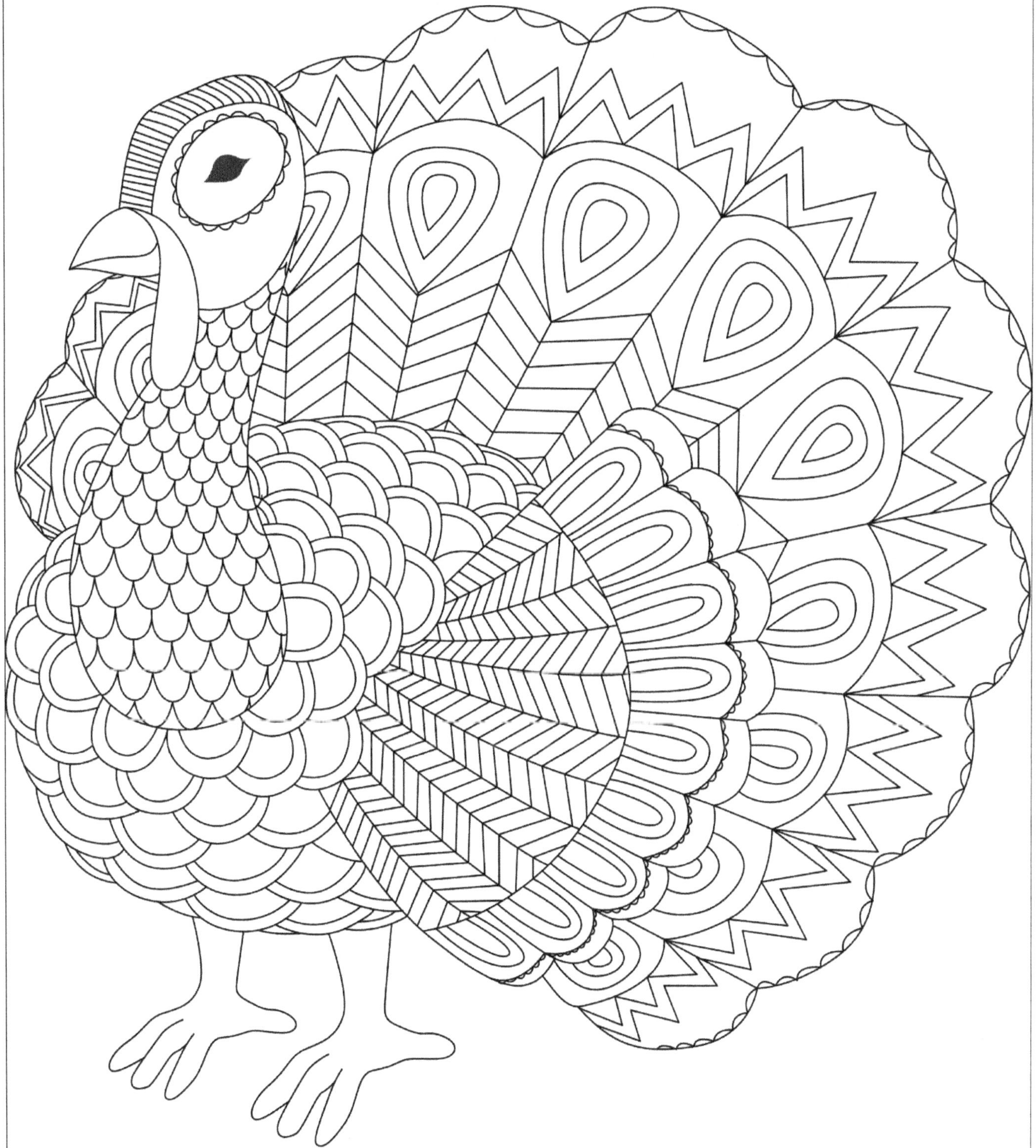

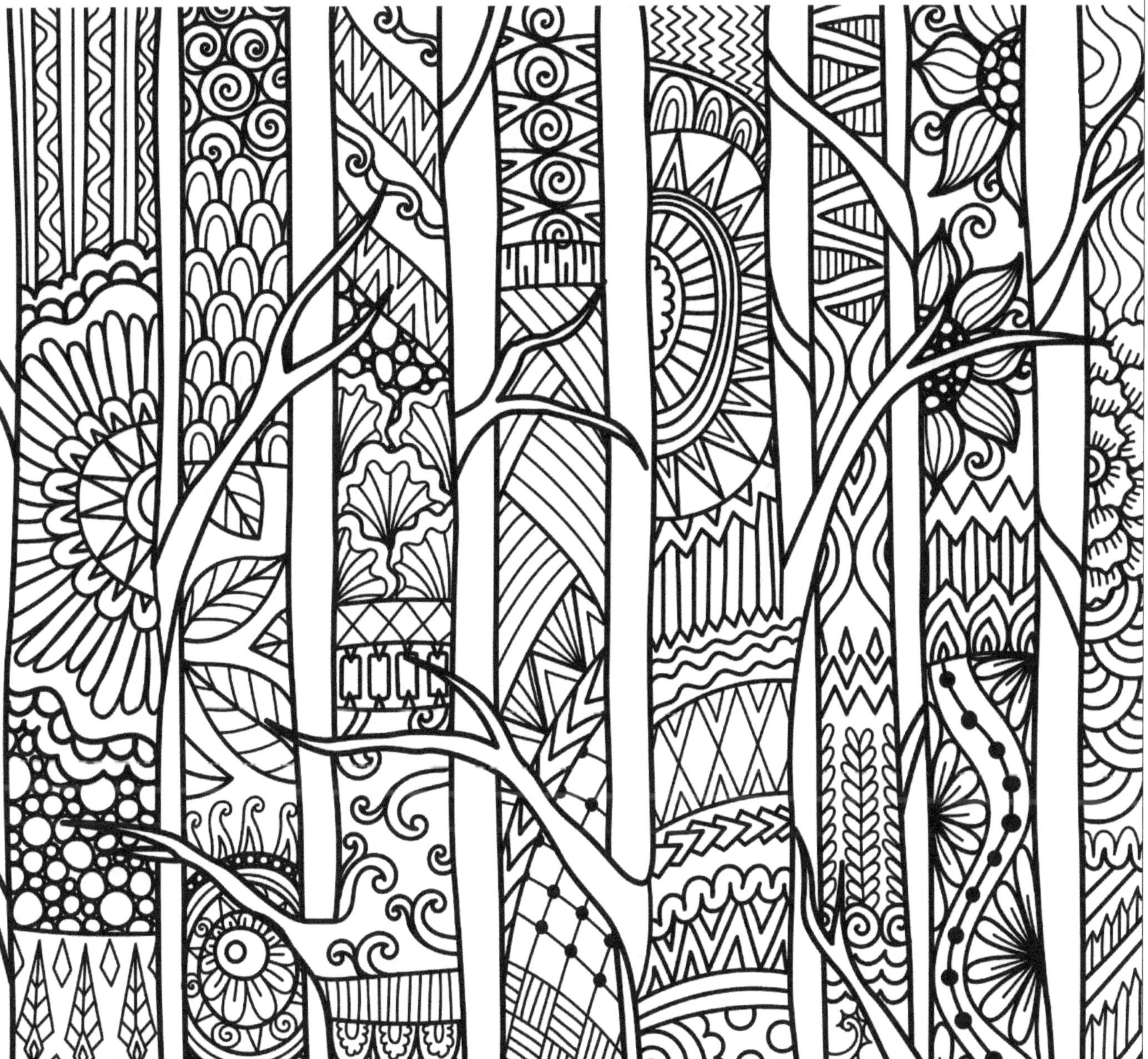

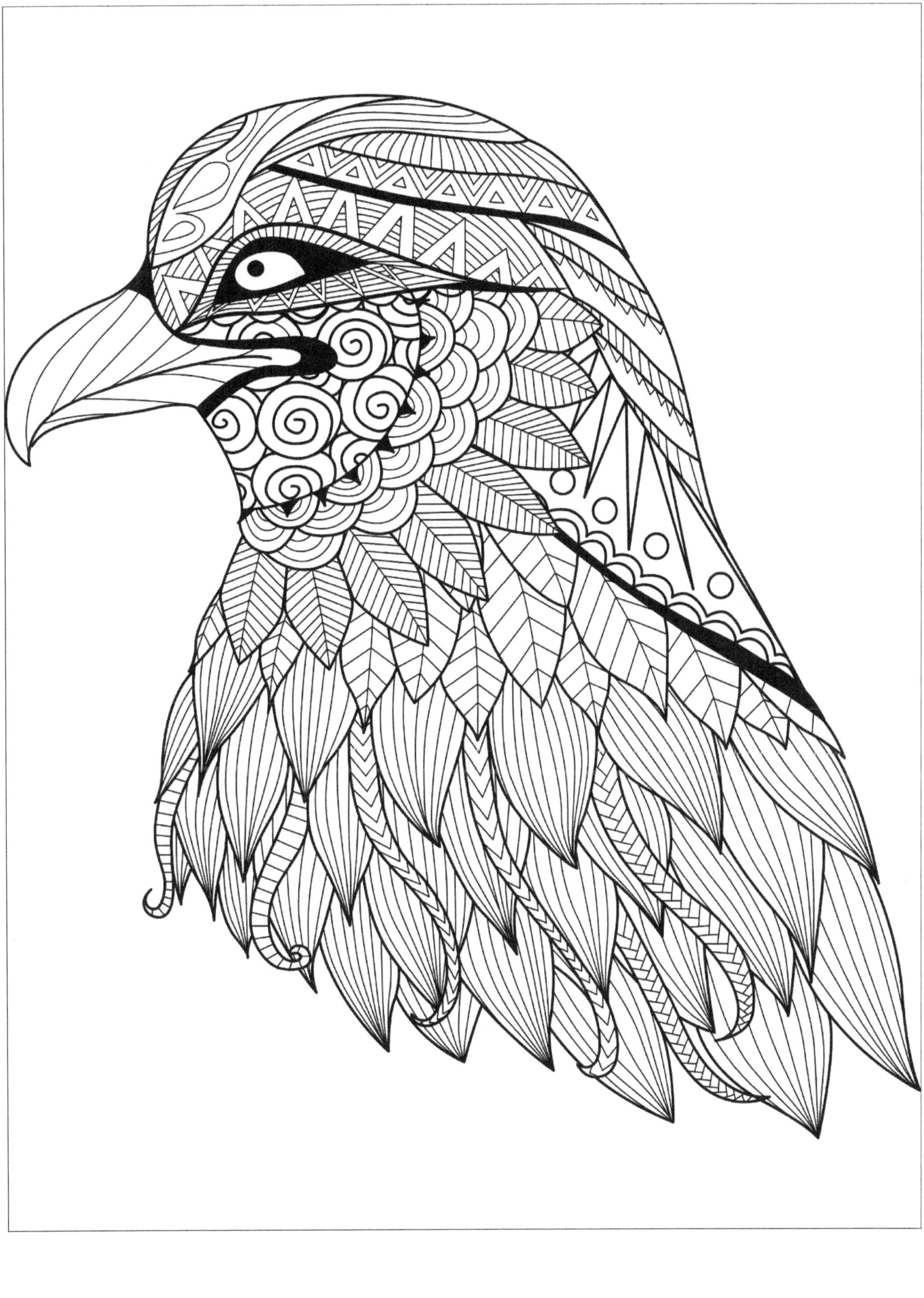

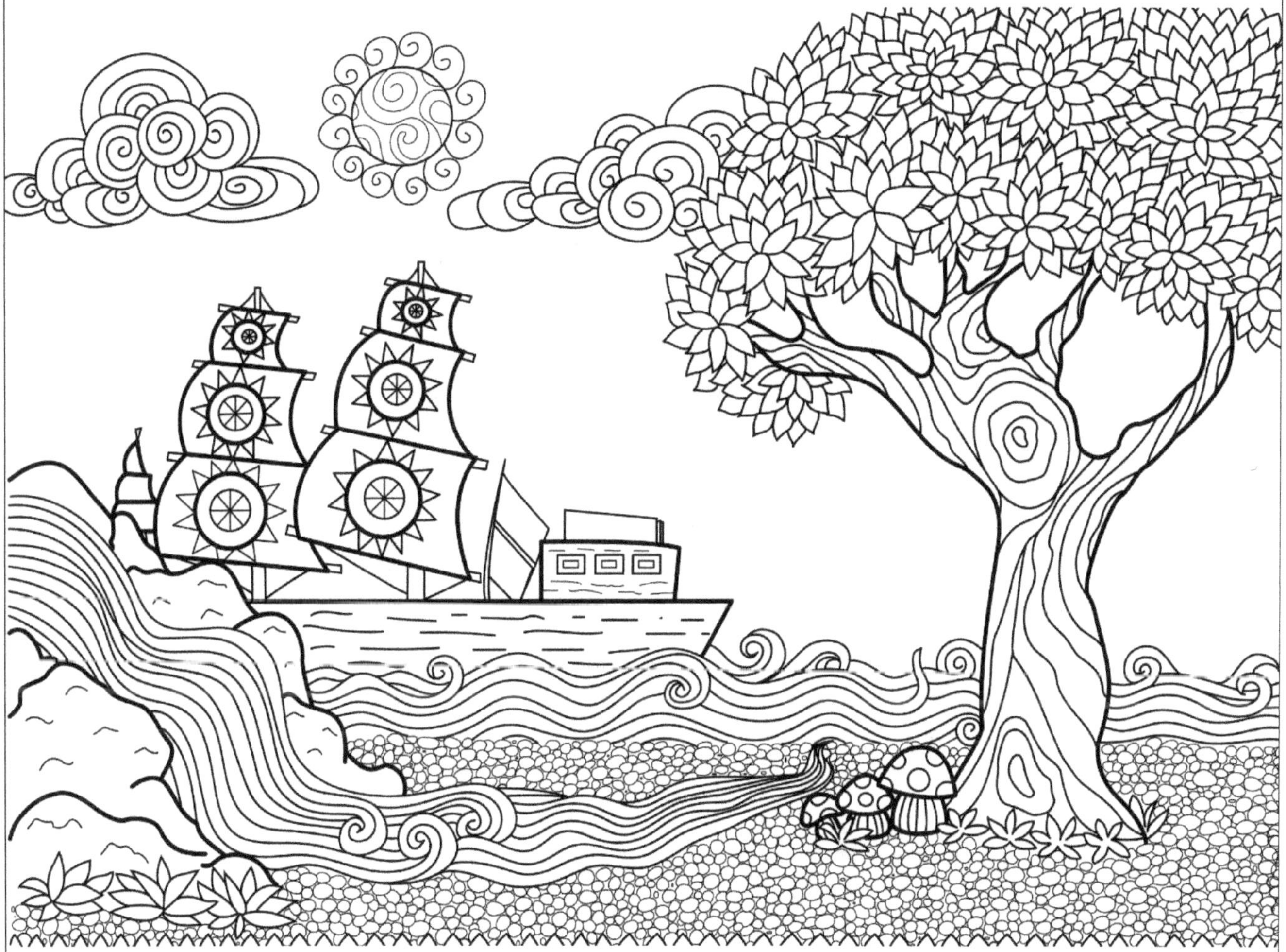

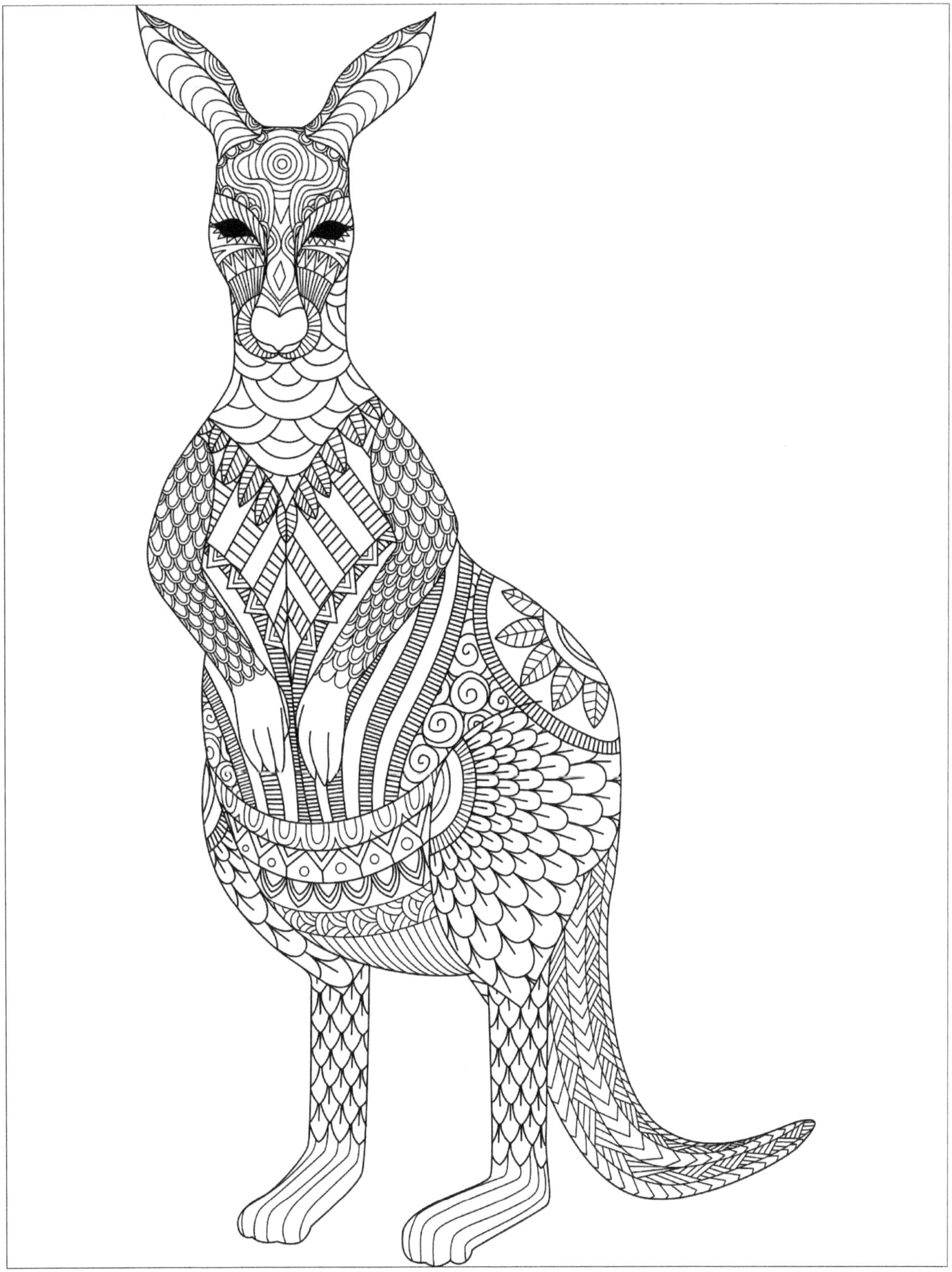

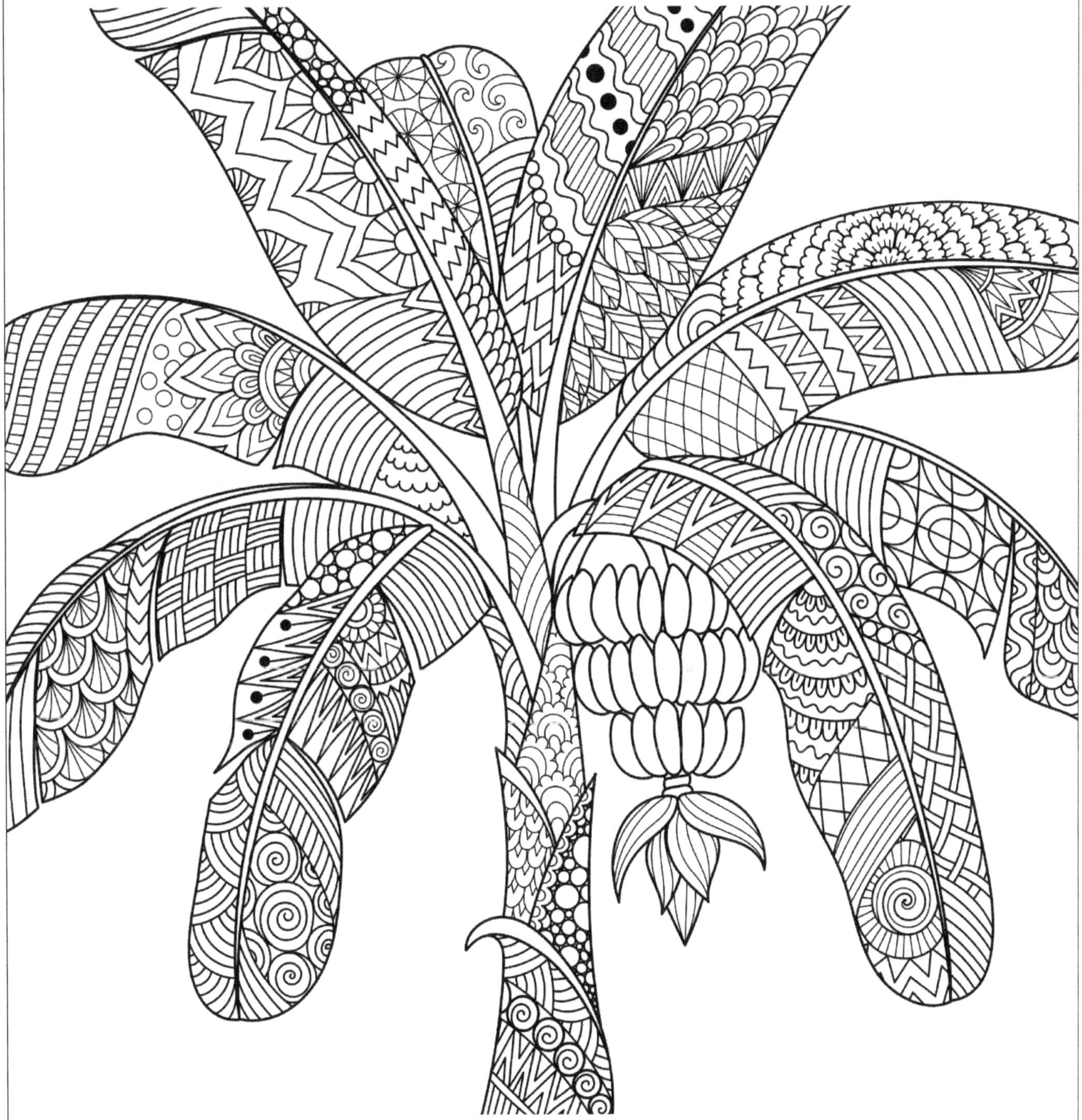

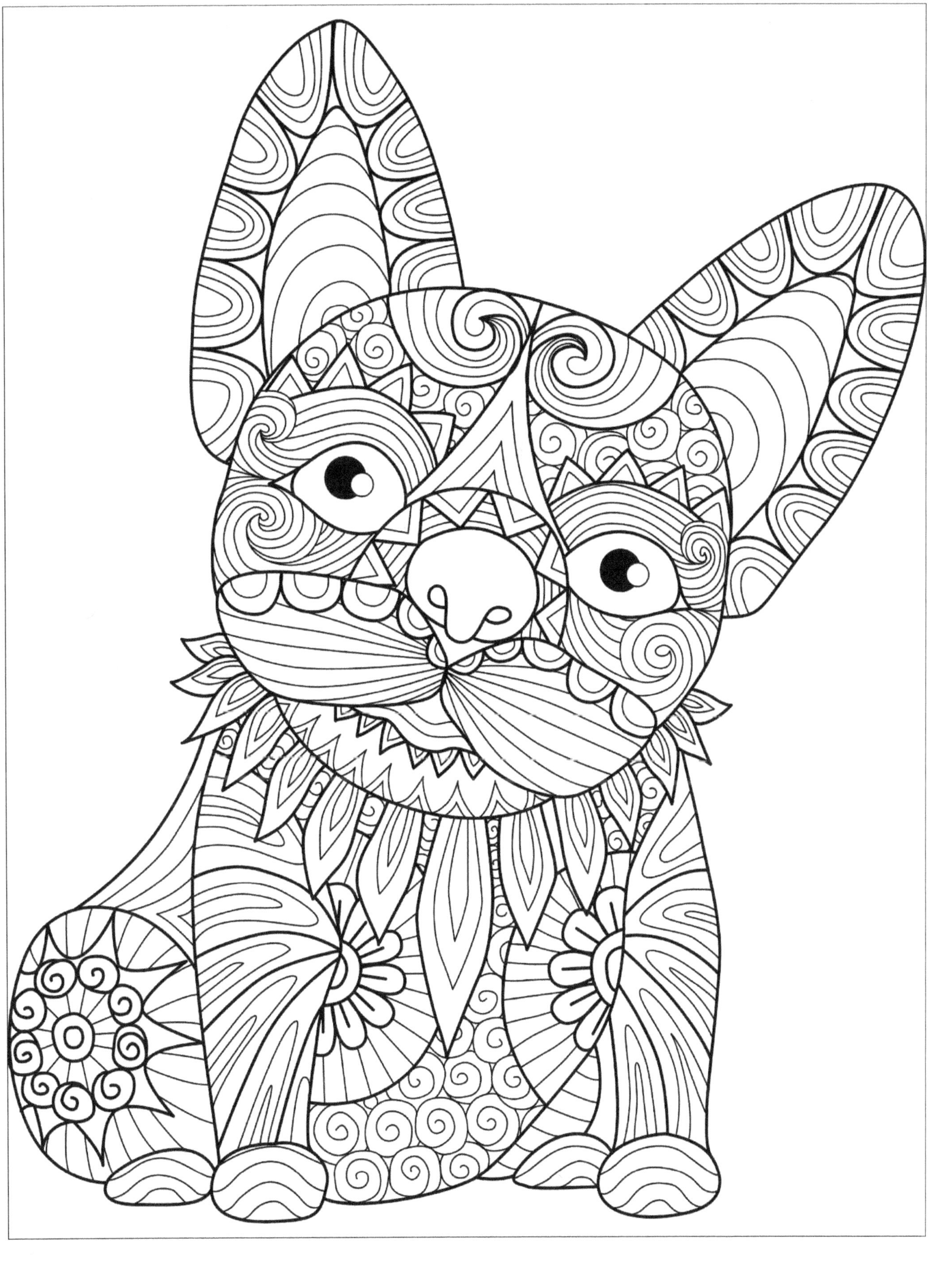

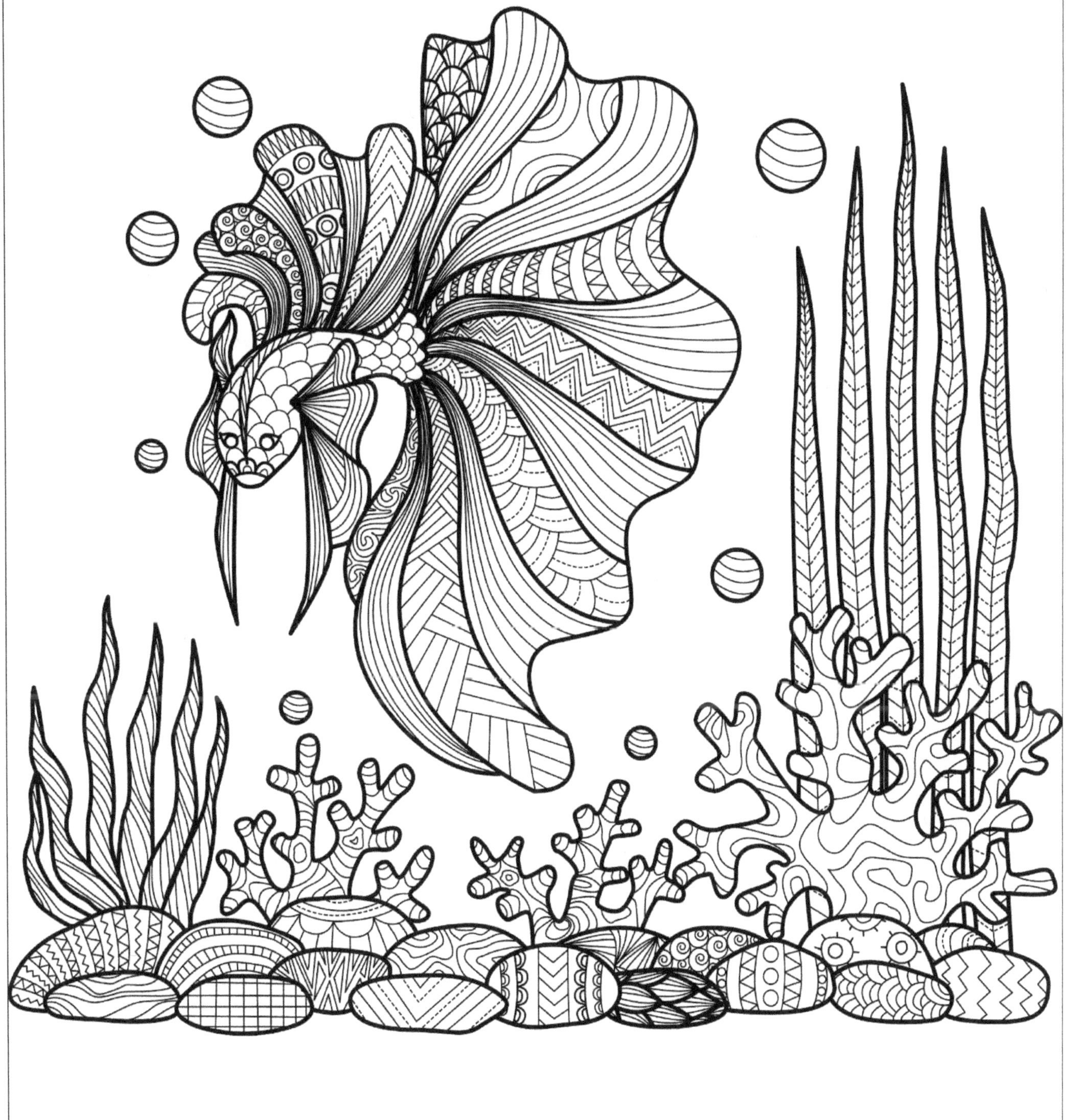

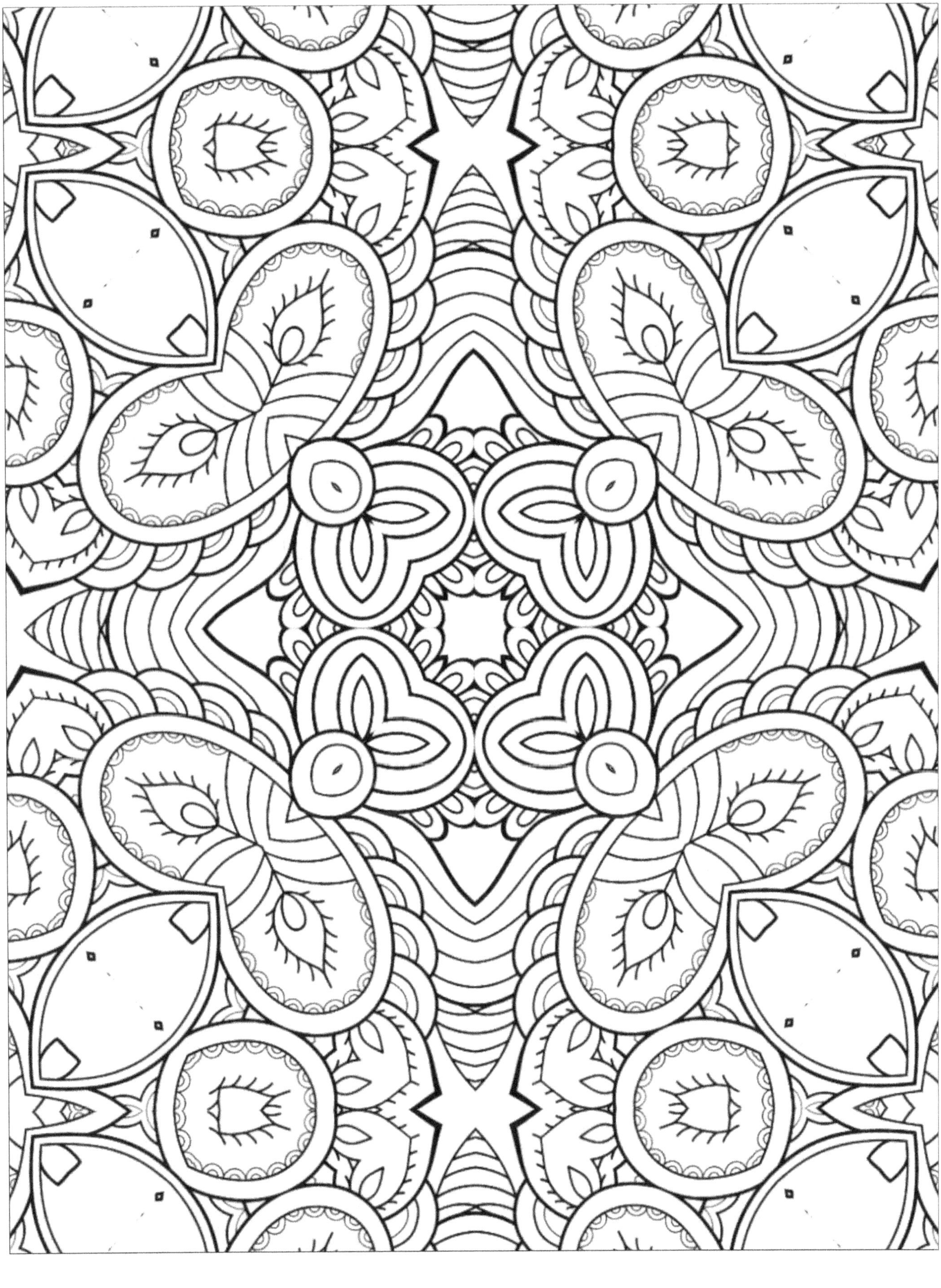

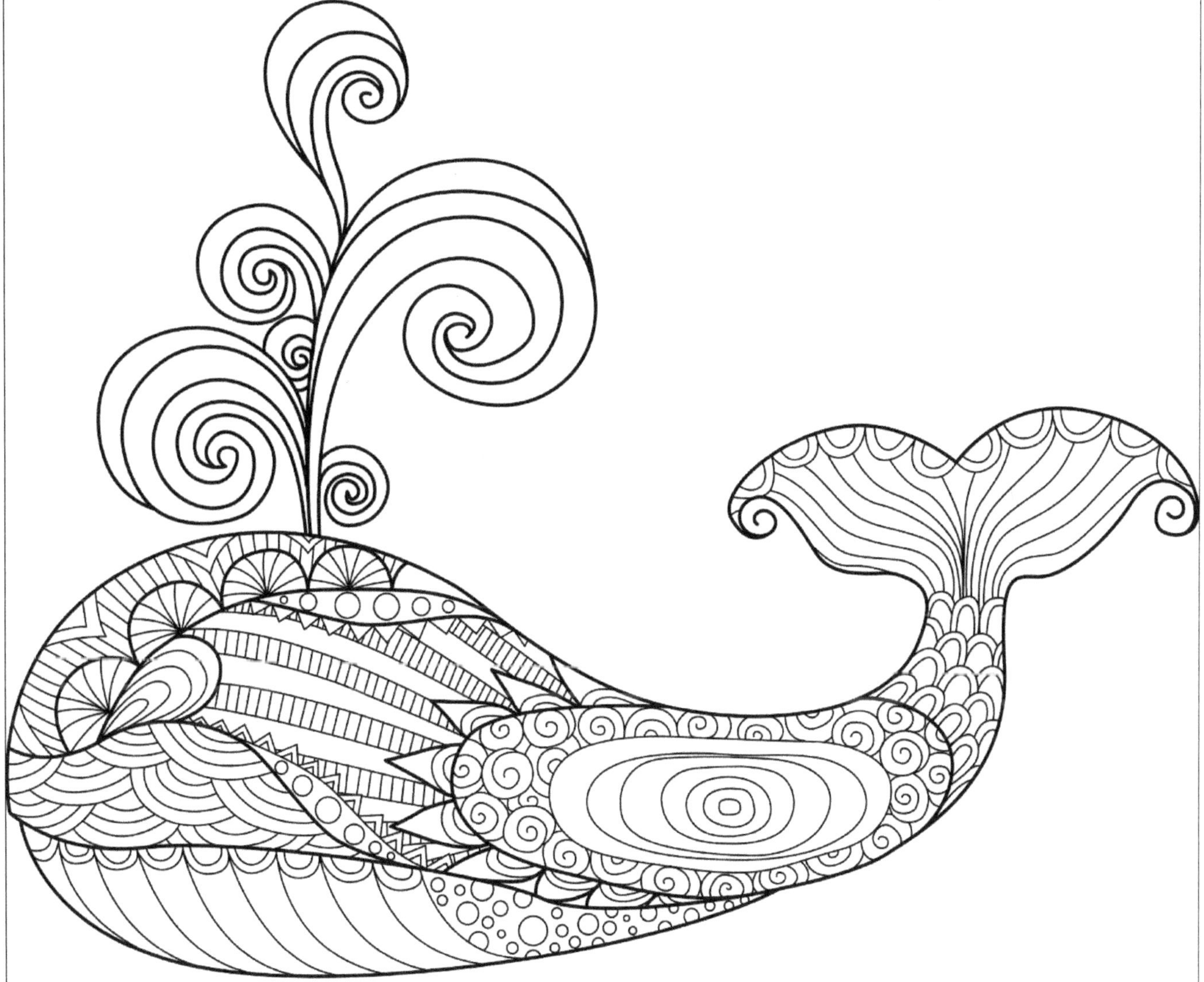

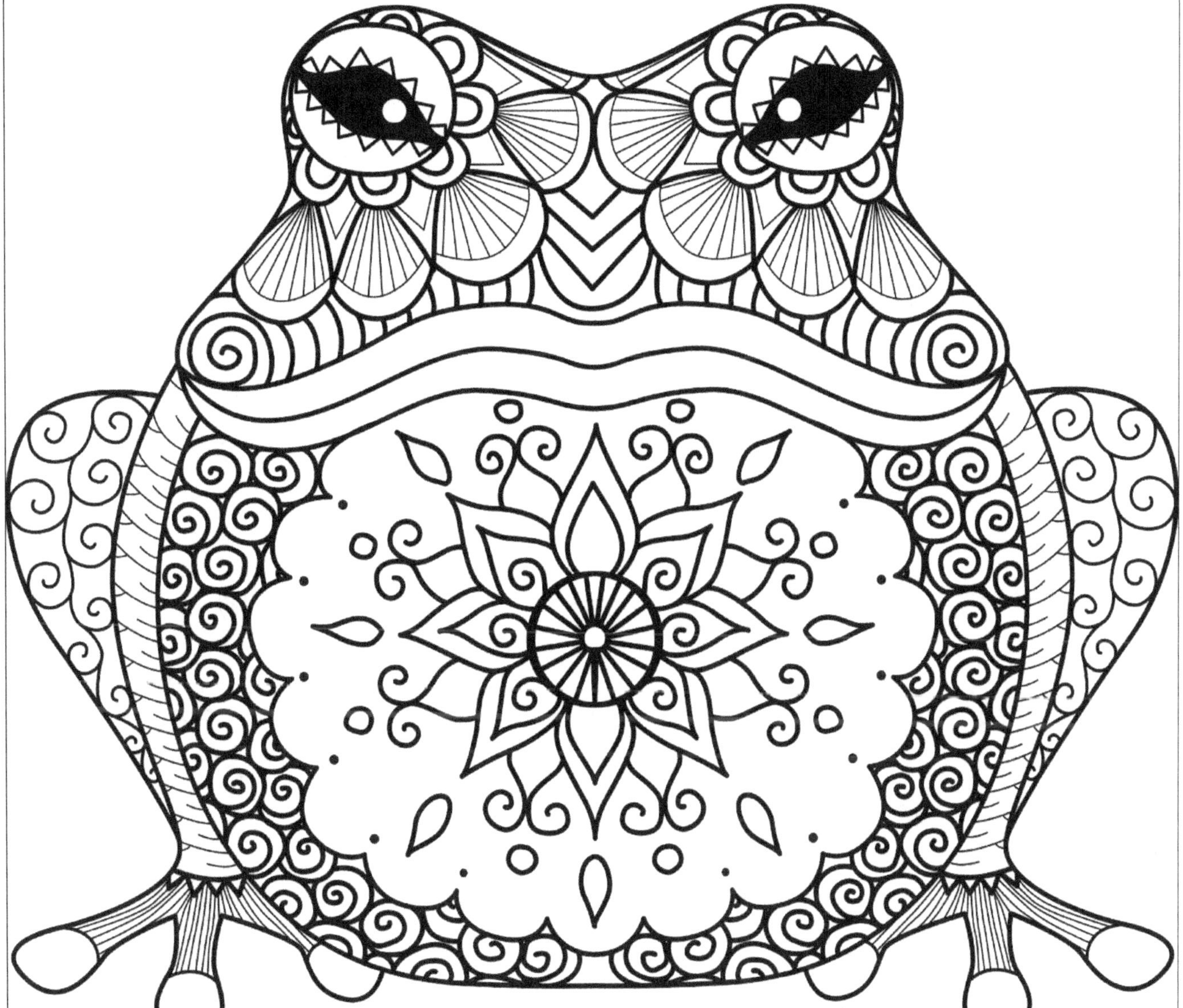

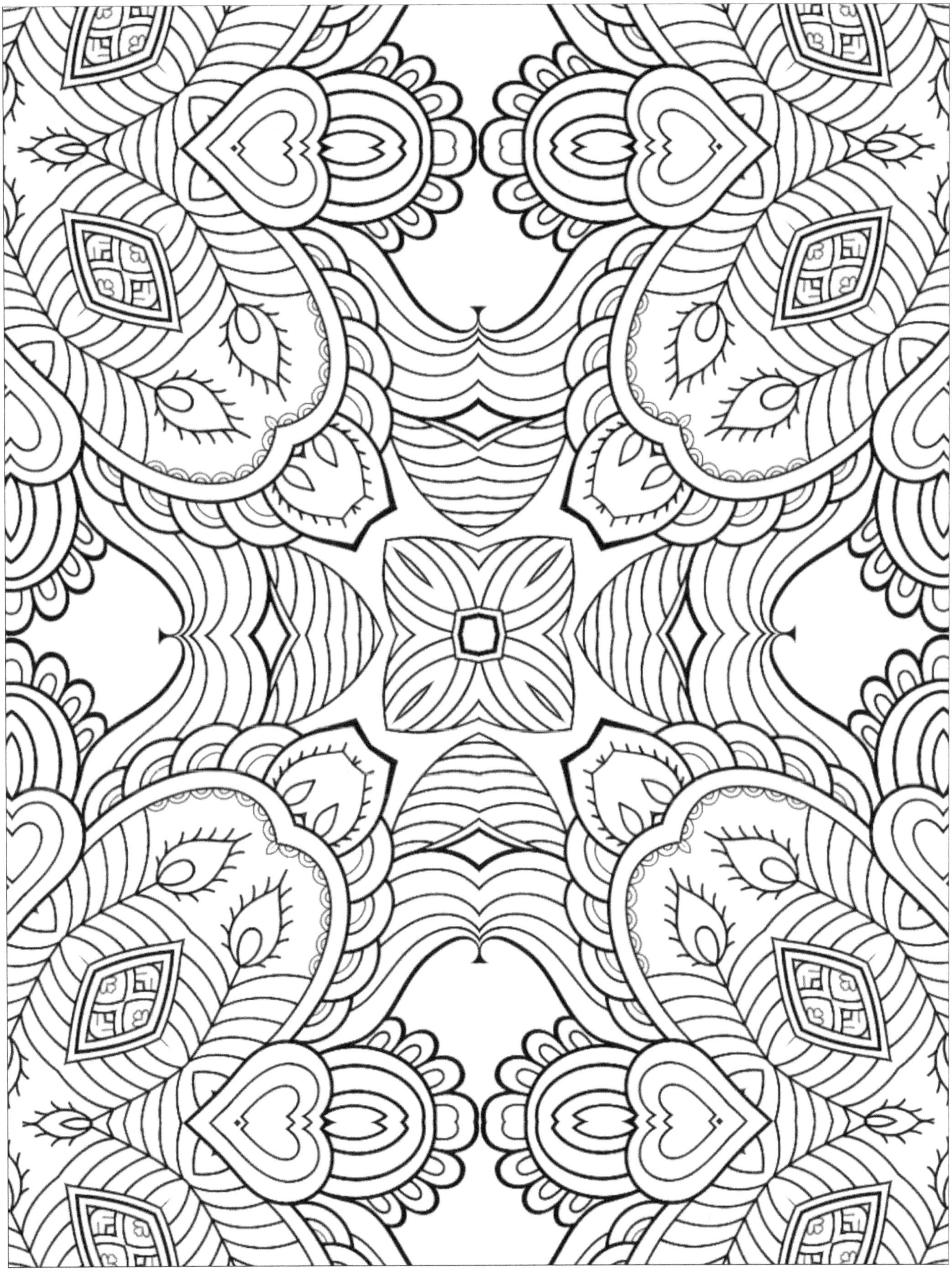

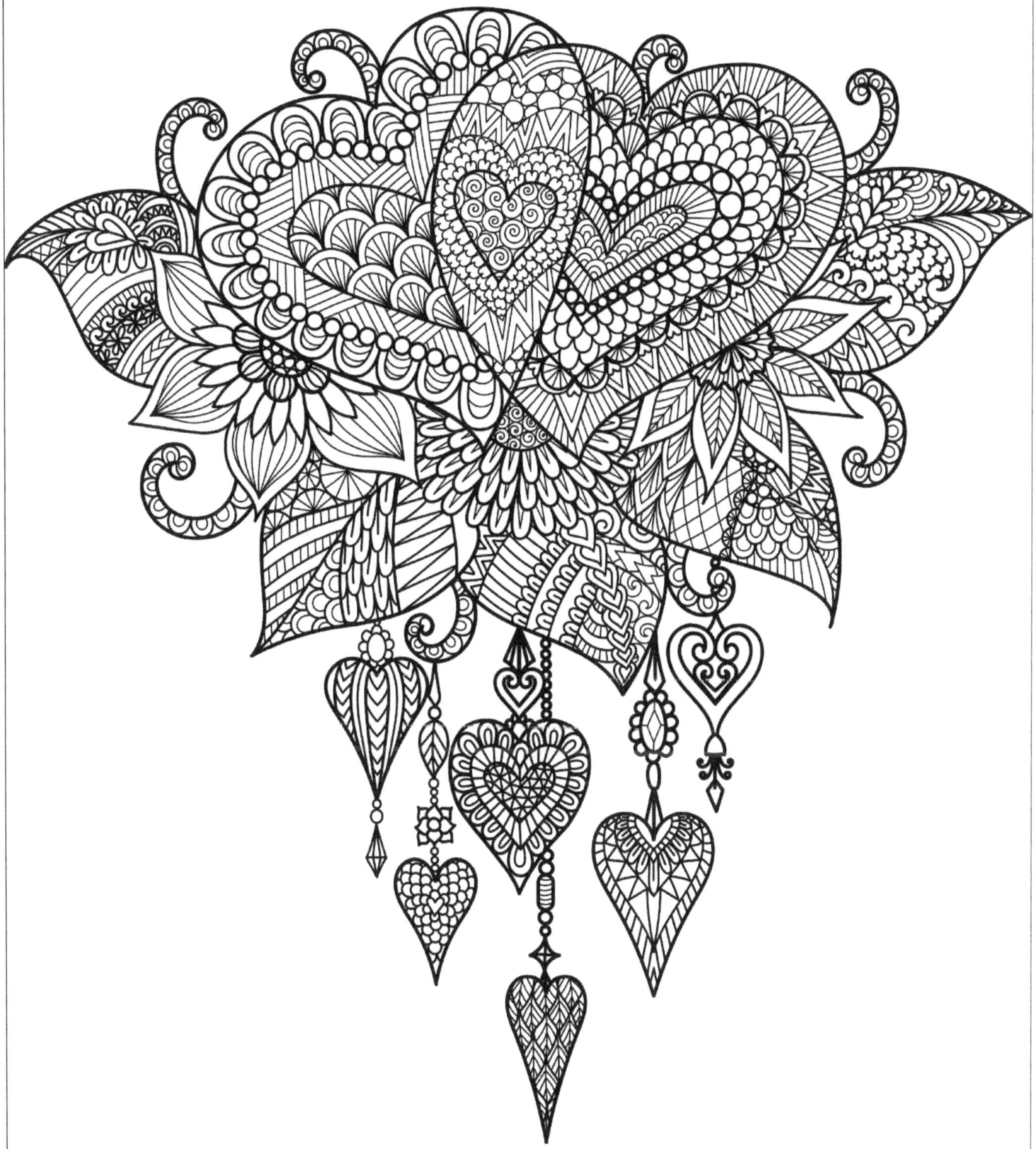

www.ingramcontent.com/pod-product-compliance
Lightning Source LLC
Chambersburg PA
CBHW082151230526
45467CB00044B/2849

* 9 7 9 8 7 0 8 9 8 9 6 6 6 *